JOHN BROOKES

THE MAN WHO INSPIRED A UNIVERSITY

JOHN HENRY BROOKES

THE MAN WHO INSPIRED A UNIVERSITY

BRYAN BROWN

Paul
with my best wishes
Bryan May 2015

OXFORD BROOKES UNIVERSITY

Editor: Susannah Baker, Oxford Brookes University
Design: Victoria Mackintosh, Oxford Brookes University

OXFORD
BROOKES
UNIVERSITY

Published in Great Britain by
Oxford Brookes University
Headington Campus, Oxford OX3 0BP

ISBN 978-0-9929299-3-0

A catalogue record for this book is held in the British Library.

Printed in Great Britain by Hunts, Kidlington, Oxfordshire.
Printed on Vision Superio 350gsm and Diamond White Triple Coated Silk 130gsm.

By the same author: *The England of Henry Taunt, Victorian Photographer,* first published in 1973 by Routledge and Kegan Paul Ltd, London

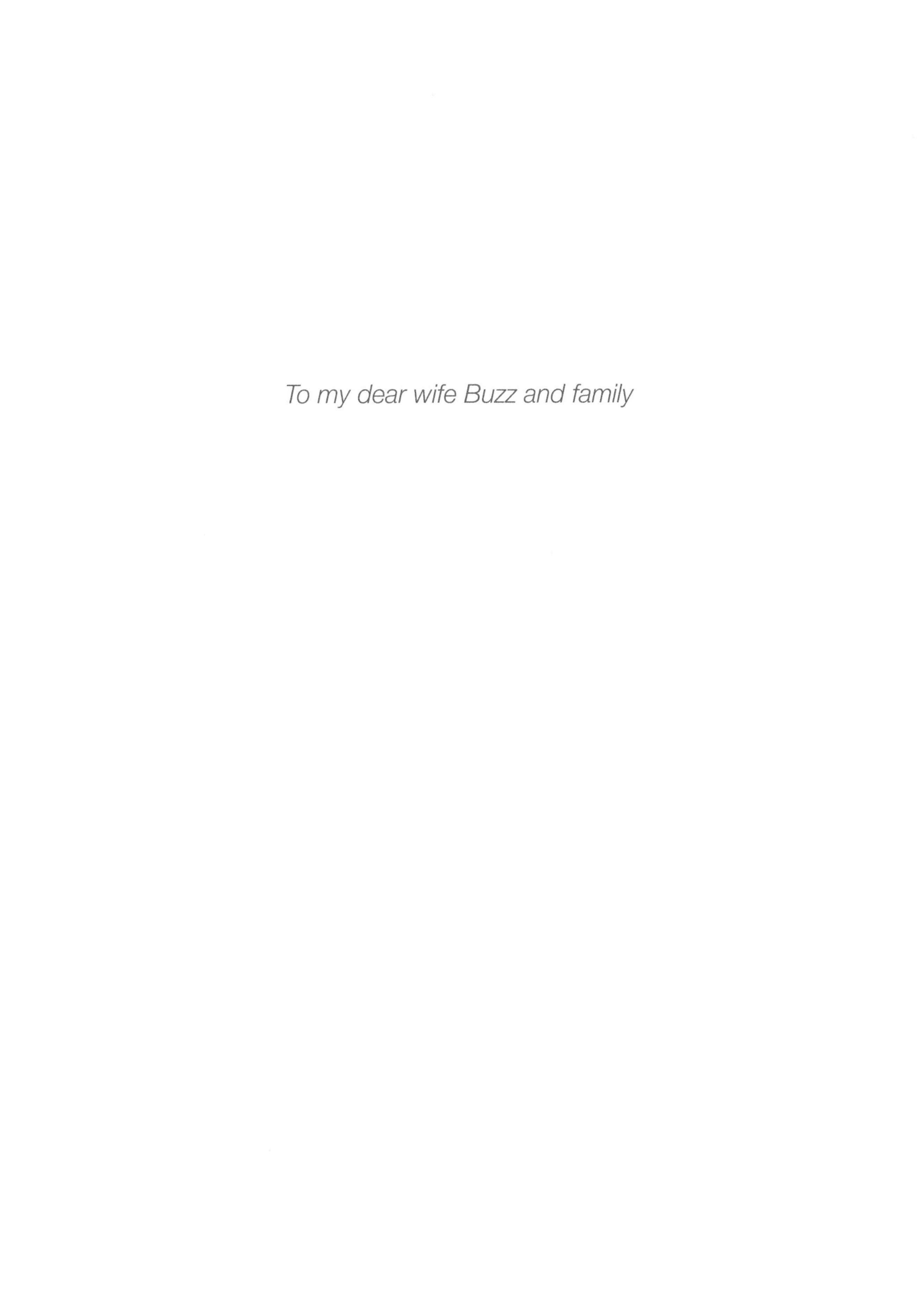

To my dear wife Buzz and family

CONTENTS

FOREWORD
Professor Janet Beer, Vice-Chancellor, Oxford Brookes University 9

PROLOGUE
An inspiring educator 11

PART ONE
THE LIFE OF JOHN HENRY BROOKES 13

The formative years: 1891 – 1928 15
A father's influence and family 16
School and college 18
The Arts and Crafts Movement and William Morris 21
The Guild of Handicraft 22
Artists and craftsmen of influence 25
Educational ideals 27
World War One 28
'Jack' the Cotswold Craftsman 29
The teacher emerges 32

The educator: 1928 – 1945 35
A difficult inheritance: inadequate premises 38
Immediate progress 39
Lifting the bar: invaluable connections 42
Art and Technology merge 44
Oxford Honour 46
The war effort 48

Realising the vision: 1945 – 1956 49
Premises crisis 51
Becoming a college of technology 57
A terrible blow 57
The Promised Land 61

An inspiring character: 1956 – 1975 63
Appreciation of his life 69

PART TWO
REFLECTIONS ON THE 40TH
ANNIVERSARY OF HIS DEATH 71

The artist and craftsman 73
The artistic endeavour 74
Artistic accomplishment 83

Reviving his legacy 87
Personal values and influence 88
A champagne moment 89

APPENDICES 92
Chronology 92
Acknowledgements 94
Sources and further reading 95
Institution titles 96
Picture credits 96
Index 97

A pen and ink drawing by John Henry Brookes of the Oxford Schools of Technology, Art and Commerce main building in Church Street, St Ebbe's, drawn in 1954.

FOREWORD

It is with great pleasure that I introduce this timely volume, *John Henry Brookes: The man who inspired a university.* As Principal of the most substantial predecessor institution to Oxford Brookes University, John Henry Brookes was a man of many talents who inspired generations of students to fulfil their ambitions in professions where their industry would be rewarded with both a sense of personal achievement and social and economic substance.

I know that I speak for my colleagues, and for our students here at Oxford Brookes, when I say that we are hugely grateful to Bryan Brown, who knew John Henry Brookes and who is a lifelong supporter of the University, for the energy and commitment that he has brought to the writing of this biography.

We asked Bryan to craft an account of the life of John Henry Brookes that would bring his career – and in particular his dedication to broadening the opportunities for education in Oxford – to the attention of a broad readership. We wanted as many people as possible to understand the incredible contribution that John Henry Brookes made to the advancement of learning in the city.

The 150th anniversary of our founding as the Oxford School of Art in 1865 is the perfect time to launch a book that celebrates both the public and the private man and his enduring legacy.

The book has gained much from the contributions of the many people who came forward with memories and stories about their encounters with John Henry Brookes. It is clear that he is still remembered with unequivocal affection and admiration and, as a new generation of students revels in the glorious new building that is named for him, we celebrate the fact that it is his bequest to us, of student-centredness, that provided the inspiration for informing the aesthetic of the design. His influence will continue to shape and define the University as it grows and develops and we will continue to find many and varied ways to express and celebrate the values and educational principles upon which he built his vision.

Professor Janet Beer
Vice-Chancellor, Oxford Brookes University
September 2007 to January 2015

CITY OF OXFORD
SECOND

PROLOGUE
AN INSPIRING EDUCATOR

A posthumous portrait in oils by Anthony Morris, member of the Royal Portrait Society and alumnus, gifted by the artist to Oxford Brookes University in 2012.

John Henry Brookes and his influence on generations of people in Oxford is a story of a belief in the importance of education and of determination, despite all hardships. It begins on 28 March 1928 when the City of Oxford Education Committee meets. On their agenda is the appointment of a Head of the Oxford School of Art.

Founded in 1865, the Oxford School of Art had experienced a precarious life. Art, technical and scientific subjects were all in demand in 1928, but in Oxford were largely taught in dilapidated premises. The School had grown little over its first sixty years, with teaching mostly in the evenings so that the people of the city could attend after their working day. The economy and politics of Oxford had been dominated by its world-famous university for centuries. Although some members of the University of Oxford understood and supported the need for vocational education for local people, the dominant social culture of that great institution did not. This lack of support had greatly impaired the progress of education in the city for those past school-leaving age.

Oxford's industrialisation was just emerging. Car manufacturing in the city had begun, creating wider economic ripples. Britain's industrial pre-eminence of the 19th century had waned. Society had endured the traumas and dramatic changes wrought by World War One; it was now witnessing the beginnings of the Great Depression, the worst economic recession since the beginning of the Industrial Revolution. Technical schools were supported and celebrated in the more industrialised cities of England.

The School of Art was part of a wider Technical School of technical, craft and art education that in most other cities would have been called a technical college. The city's Education Committee was just beginning to realise the value that such teaching could have in the local industrial economy. Perhaps they sensed the need for some stimulus for further education in the city. They were certainly provoked by a far-sighted Secretary, Mr A C Cameron. He set out the context for the appointment of a Head of the School of Art in a remarkably prophetic statement:

> *"It is clear that the post will provide considerable scope to a man with initiative and organising power. Indeed, if the new Head shows himself to be really the right man, it may influence the future organisation of the whole system of continued education in the City."*

The committee subsequently agreed to an advertisement for the Head of the Art School – or more correctly School of Arts and Crafts – who would also act as Vice-Principal of the Oxford City Technical School. The salary was £550 to £600 per annum according to experience.

John Henry Brookes, then aged 37, was appointed to the post. He would go on to become Principal of the Oxford Schools of Technology, Art and Commerce when they combined in 1934, and would so profoundly affect education in the city of Oxford that he was awarded an honorary degree by the University of Oxford within seven years of his appointment. Later still he would have a university named in his honour.

John Henry Brookes was known to his family as Jack but often called JHB by friends and colleagues, and I have adopted this informality throughout the book. JHB had very relevant experience for the Oxford position. He was skilled in arts and crafts and had spent time working as a craftsman in the Cotswolds. He had trained as a teacher in Leicester. At the time of his application, he was teaching both at a Yorkshire grammar school and part-time at the University of Sheffield. Perhaps crucially though, he already knew Oxford and the School of Art through a temporary teaching position in the early 1920s.

Some fifty years later, then Secretary to the Oxford Education Committee, John Garne, confirmed his predecessor's earlier prediction:

> *"John Brookes was the constant source of inspiration in promoting the development of further and adult education in the city for thirty years."*

The two secretaries foresaw and acknowledged a remarkable achievement. At first glance, JHB seems an unlikely candidate as a role model: small in stature, gentle and unassuming. His former colleague, Head of the School of Commerce, A Edward Jenkinson, explains:

> *"It seems surprising that such a modest man could have been consistently successful in the many varied projects he undertook. I believe that the explanation is that he knew instinctively how to deal with people – the human aspect."*

He could be considered a renaissance man, a man of many gifts: creativity, organising ability, a love of humanity, a great sense of humour and a craftsman in all he did. As with most accomplished leaders, he was a sound judge of character. He had an innate ability to deal with all kinds of people, but with it a steely drive and determination.

JHB's educational inspiration had a profound effect on generations of people in Oxford. His vision would lay firm foundations for what was to become Oxford Brookes University. During his twenty-eight years, most of the fields of study offered by the University in the 21st century were established and began to win national recognition.

He would also be instrumental in the foundations of Southfield School in 1934 (now Oxford Spires Academy), Cheney School, which opened in 1954 (now also an academy), and the Oxford College of Further Education (now City of Oxford College) in 1961.

To mastermind the formative years of a university, a college of further education, and two secondary schools is all the more impressive in the historical context: the Great Depression of the late 1920s and 1930s, through World War Two and its deprived aftermath, until the glimmer of recovery in the 1950s. It was an outstanding achievement, the nature of which is perhaps unparalleled in British education.

Like so many young people in Oxford, my education was shaped by his ideals as well as his teaching more directly. Over the past few years I have grown to understand the huge debt of gratitude that I, and many others, owe to John Henry Brookes. My aim is to shed light on JHB's life and educational ideas, and to explain why the University has taken his name. I hope this book will go some way towards repaying the gratitude that is due.

Bryan Brown, Abingdon-on-Thames, Oxfordshire
January 2015

PART ONE
THE LIFE OF JOHN HENRY BROOKES

THE FORMATIVE YEARS
1891 – 1928

Previous page: A studio photograph of the Brookes family in the late 1890s: father Robert, mother Annie, sister Margaret and JHB.

THE FORMATIVE YEARS 1891 – 1928

John Henry Brookes was born in Northampton on 31 January 1891, into a super-confident Victorian Britain, with significant economic and political power based on a burgeoning Empire. Indeed it was the most powerful nation in the world. This was an era of invention and discovery with significant developments in science and technology, resulting in the huge growth in manufacturing. Advances in medicine led to a dramatic growth in population that fuelled urbanisation. Railroads provided the first major advancement in land transportation for centuries, changing the way people lived and traded.

Northampton had grown dramatically in the 19th century, following the creation of the Grand Union Canal and the arrival of railways. A key industry was the manufacture of boots and shoes, a development from leather goods manufacturing of the 18th century.

A FATHER'S INFLUENCE AND FAMILY

John Henry Brookes, or JHB as he was widely known to friends and colleagues, was the only son of Robert Henry Brookes and his wife Annie Watts, née Dykes. The Brookes family had been Midlands-based for generations, coming from Birmingham, Leicester and Northampton. The Dykes family originated from Scotland; Annie's forebears moved to Northampton no doubt for work, and were associated with the radical politics and religious non-conformism that the town was known for in the 19th century. The family tree, which JHB drew in his retirement years, records that teaching and craftsmanship extended back over four generations of both families.

JHB's career was perhaps mapped genetically but his success would be hard won. Robert and Annie were of typical artisan stock. They embraced strong Christian values and were members of the Congregational Church, believed in the importance of family life and enjoyed many homely musical evenings with Robert playing the flute and leading the singing. So the young John and his sister Margaret were raised in a loving and secure family. On Robert and Annie's wedding certificate of 1889, Robert's occupation is Foreman Boot Clicker. This was one of the most skilled craft jobs in Northampton's successful footwear trade. A boot clicker cut the uppers for boots and shoes from a prepared hide, maximising the number of uppers that could be cut from one piece of leather and avoiding the thin areas. This was a well-paid job deriving its name from the noise the knife made on a wooden board when it cut through the leather.

Robert was a major influence on his son and many of his attitudes, beliefs and values guided JHB throughout his life. Extracts from Robert's obituaries of 1938 and other press cuttings commenting on his career progress, give a clear picture:

> *"Mr (Robert) Brookes was no self advertiser. He never sought the limelight or the praise of men. He was anxious only that his work should be well done and to that end he brought a patience, energy and conscientiousness which allied with great ability, brought him triumphantly to his goal."*

> *"He was a man of noble ideals and set himself a high standard of performance. As a personality he was quiet, humble and thoughtful or to put it in more dramatic terms; there is nothing of the electro – plate, requiring constant polish, about Mr Brookes. He is true metal all through. There is no straighter man ever walked than Robert Brookes."*

Father and son seem to have had very similar personalities: similar words and sentiments would be used about JHB in his later years.

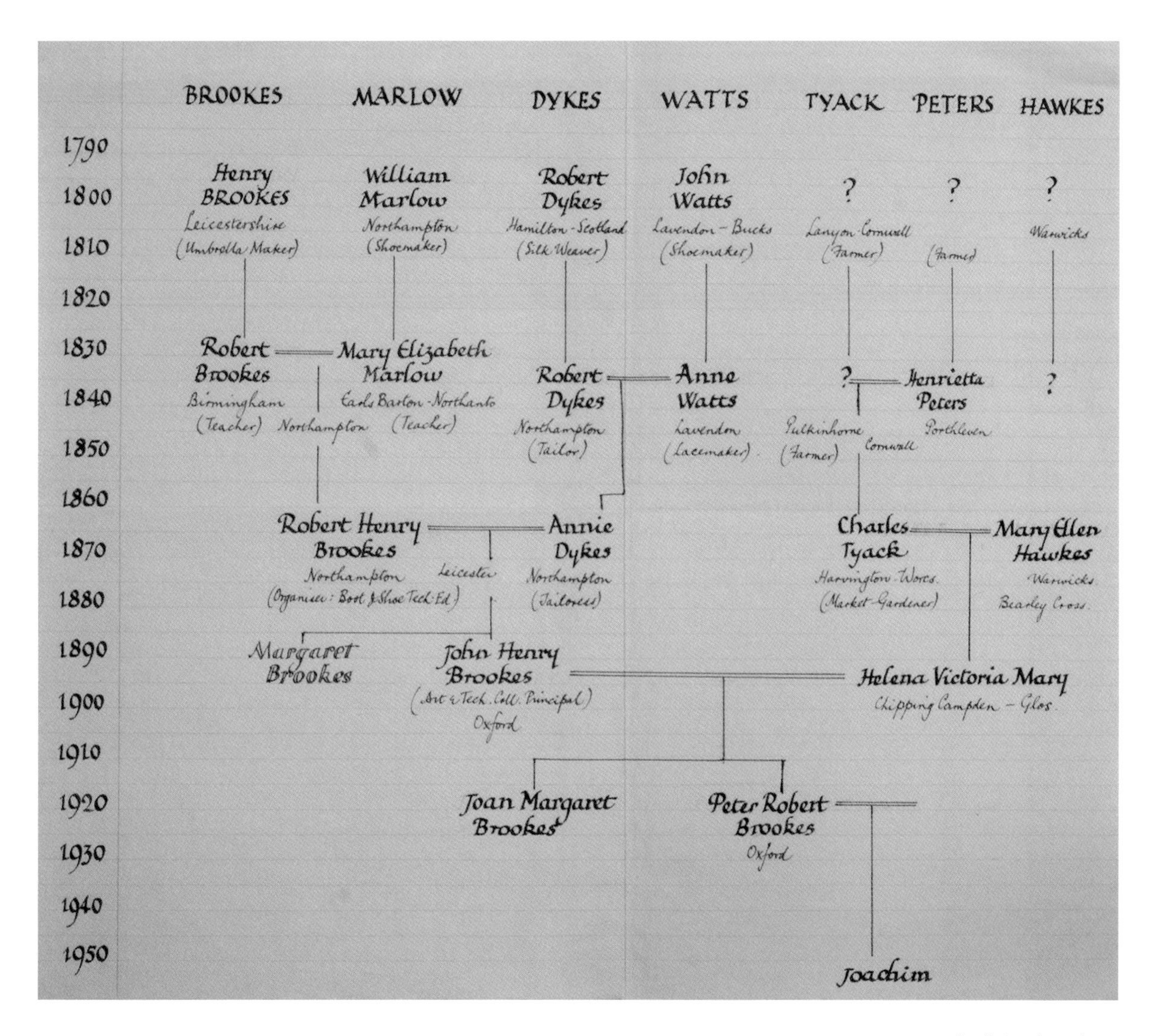

Family tree drawn by JHB in his retirement years.

A group of day students and staff from the Art School, Leicester Municipal Technical and Art School which JHB attended from 1909 to 1916. JHB is standing in the second row from the front, second from the left; Benjamin J Fletcher (1868-1951), Head of the School is seated centrally in the second row, sixth from the left and (John) Sydney Reeve is standing on the far right. The photograph is taken c1915.

Opposite: A watercolour plant study of Lapageria rosea alba made by JHB in 1909 when he was a first year art student.

SCHOOL AND COLLEGE

JHB showed early promise and in September 1903, he went to Northampton Grammar School. His artistic interests emerged early. He read the Bible with his widowed grandmother, enjoying the illustrations by the French artist and engraver, Paul Gustave Doré, in an 1866 edition. He recalled, *"I never tired of the drawings which seemed incredibly skilful; I had great admiration of the engravings."* In later life, JHB, gifted with a photographic memory, would be able to recreate the Doré engravings from these early memories.

In 1905 Robert Brookes decided to make a career change and move from industry into education. He took up the position of Head of the Boot and Shoe Department at Leicester Municipal Technical and Art School. JHB writes, *"My father moved into education with a missionary zeal, from that moment the whole family became indoctrinated."*

The family moved from Northampton to Leicester and JHB transferred to Wyggeston Grammar School for Boys, where he won prizes for both academic and artistic work. Leicester, like Northampton, had grown significantly in the 19th century, with new industries such as engineering, hosiery and textiles, and with an emerging boot and shoe manufacturing sector.

After Wyggeston Grammar, JHB moved on to the Leicester Municipal Training College in September 1907 to continue with his general education. His artistic and craft abilities were coming to the fore, no doubt encouraged by his father's commitment to craftsmanship, and in 1909 he enrolled at the Leicester School of Art. It seems that he followed a broadly based art and design course that included drawing and painting, graphics, a wide range of craft work, and history of art and architecture. JHB was able and interested in lettering and typography, and he made a particular study of these subjects.

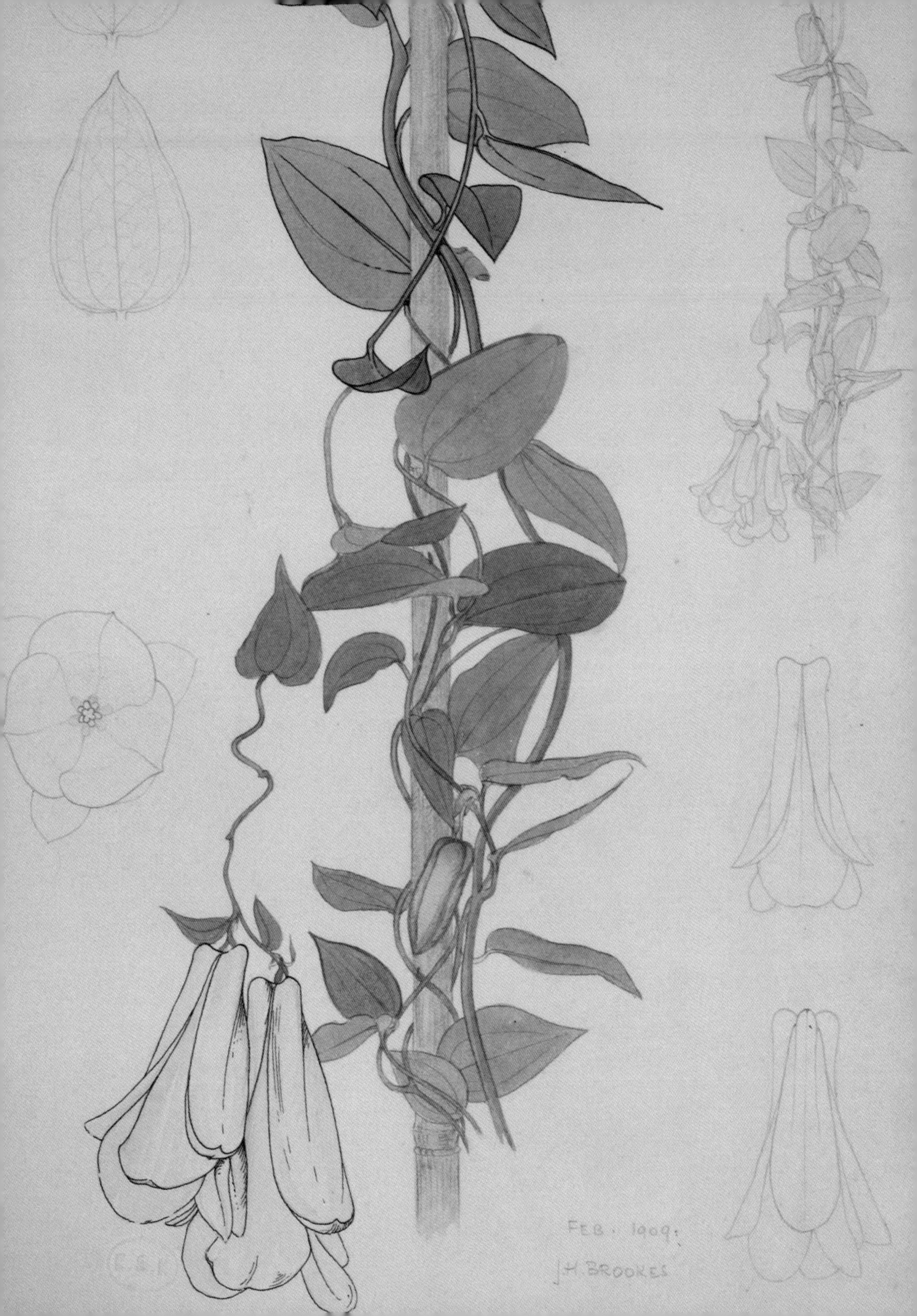
FEB. 1909.
J.H. BROOKES

JHB lived, studied and taught in Leicester until he was 25 years old. He came into contact with people who would have a significant influence on his own thinking, and who would evolve the development of design in 20th century Britain. His working knowledge of the interaction between the town's industrial and educational activities helped shape his educational philosophies and ideas.

Opposite: A male head c1914, arguably JHB's finest pencil drawing during his student years.

THE ARTS AND CRAFTS MOVEMENT AND WILLIAM MORRIS

During his teenage years the next major influence on his life, evolving from his father's interests, becomes apparent. It was the Arts and Crafts Movement, perhaps the most important and influential artistic and social movement to emerge from England for 250 years. The Movement was inspired by the writings of thinkers and intellectuals, including Thomas Carlyle and significantly John Ruskin. JHB as a young art student absorbed these ideas voraciously, but the more important influence was William Morris and his circle. Writing years later he put it succinctly:

> *"A craft student working in the early years of this century* (20th century) *was naturally deeply impressed by the work of William Morris. His influence remains with me and is most probably as compulsive today as it was 50 years ago."*

The Movement was at the height of its influence between 1880 and 1910 but its ideas prevailed well into the 20th century. It emerged from a group of young London-based architects who founded The Art Workers' Guild in 1884, to break down the barriers between architects, artists, applied artists/designers and craftsmen/makers. An offshoot, The Arts and Crafts Exhibition Society set up in 1888, brought together this artistic grouping and importantly included manufacturers. This held great meaning for JHB, particularly the relationship with industry. It also heralded the emergence of design as a profession, which developed and flourished over the next century.

In its simplest terms the Arts and Crafts Movement was based on functional forms, on clean lines, truth to materials and the use of nature as the source for all pattern. It was a reaction against the Victorian fashion for overly complex design. But the Movement also had a social momentum, aimed at reversing the effects of the Industrial Revolution and the debasement of the role of work. Its founders had a conviction that art and craft could change people's lives. Earlier Victorian society believed happiness was created from economic progress; by the 1880s this conviction was being threatened. Religious standards and social values were challenged by the writings of Thomas Paine, Robert Owen and Charles Darwin. Agricultural production was in decline, urban industrialisation was leading to deep class divisions and the degradation of much of the workforce. The term 'unemployment' entered the vocabulary. Journalists wrote of grim living conditions in the cities and the Bloody Sunday demonstration in London in 1887 raised the prospect of political revolution.

So the Movement inspired changes in many aspects of society. They included the beginnings of the Labour movement and the Fabian Society; community life through the Garden City Movement and the development of Letchworth in 1903; conservation and the formation of organisations like the National Trust. The Movement also led to the emergence of working women like Morris's daughter May and the garden designer Gertrude Jekyll, and had impact on other artistic activities such as music inspired by rural surroundings expressed by composers including Cecil Sharp and Ralph Vaughan Williams. Its reach was profound.

William Morris championed the value of work to the labourer, the producer and the consumer. Morris's interests in communal life and a 'simple life' in the country, based on medieval crafts and guilds, significantly influenced JHB.

Morris also expressed a romantic idealisation of craftsmen, taking pride in their handiwork and giving it a higher moral worth than machine production. Although he initially subscribed to this, JHB tempered his attitudes as he grew older. He was not a middle-class idealist like the founders of the Movement, but the son of a skilled tradesman. He too would be a champion of the value of human work, but he also knew the significance of manufacturing to economic well-being, and would ensure that the education he led was close to the world of work.

Right: A portrait of William Morris (1834-1896) by William Hollyer 1884.

Far right: Charles Ashbee (1863-1942) photographed by his friend the eminent American architect, Frank Lloyd Wright in 1900.

THE GUILD OF HANDICRAFT

In 1913, the Arts and Crafts Movement became a more direct influence on JHB, then aged 22. In the summer holidays he and a fellow student had visited the theatre at Stratford-on-Avon. In his own words, writing in 1967:

> *"We afterwards decided to cycle out to Chipping Campden, a place unknown to me except by repute as the home of the Guild of Handicraft. I remembered that we rode slowly the length of its High Street. I was entranced and I said to my companion: this is where I would like to live, work and die. Later I achieved the first two of these objectives and today I'm not greatly concerned about the third. The day's visit lengthened to a month of pleasurable craftsmanship."*

The Guild of Handicraft was the brainchild of another wealthy, middle-class idealist, the multi-skilled architect, furniture designer and silversmith, Charles Ashbee. He established the Guild in 1888 in Toynbee Hall, Whitechapel in London's East End, moving it to workshops at Essex House in Mile End with his partner, the noted architect Mackay Hugh Baillie Scott. Their mission statement was:

> *'To seek not only to set a higher standard of craftsmanship, but at the same time, and in so doing, to protect the status of the craftsman. To this end it endeavours to steer a mean between the independence of the artist - which is individualistic and often parasitical - and the trade shop, where the workman is bound to purely commercial and antiquated traditions and has, as a rule, neither stake in the business nor any interest beyond his weekly wage'.*

The Guild, along with the Glasgow School and the nearby Cotswold School, are among the best known Arts and Crafts branches that followed on from William Morris's leadership. At its core was the medieval idea of artistic communities, where artists and craftsmen lived and worked together. The wide reach of the Movement embraced the setting up of local societies, exhibitions, and teaching handicrafts and art at schools and evening classes. They were driven by Ruskin and Morris's high minded ideals of establishing community craft industries, supported by socialist ideas of regenerating rural communities often where industry had declined. The craft revival was stimulated by the leading art schools that were pioneering applied art. They engaged with local industries, training local artisans and spreading the development of art and craft education.

The Arts and Crafts Movement engaged an increasingly wide range of artists, architects and the emerging applied artists, designers of furniture, ceramics, books, household and decorative products. They included architect designers such as Charles Voysey, ceramicists like William de Morgan and William Moorcroft, furniture designers like Edward Barnsley and Ernest Gimson, who influenced new design-conscious retailers like Liberty, and Heal and Son.

Ashbee visualised a sylvan setting for his craftsmen, influenced no doubt by Morris's move to Kelmscott Manor in Oxfordshire, the Cotswold School and other rural groups. So in 1902, after reviewing a number of choices, Ashbee and the Guildsmen made the bold decision to improve the quality of their lives by moving some fifty of them to Chipping Campden in the centre of the Cotswolds. Although Ashbee was the founder of the Guild, it was a decision based on a democratic vote of the Guildsmen who included jewellers, enamellers, wood carvers, cabinet makers, silversmiths, French polishers, book binders, printers, carpenters and blacksmiths. On hearing the result of the vote, Ashbee wrote in his journal:

> *"I am glad to think that the men themselves have decided on the whole it is better to leave Babylon and go home to the land."*

Chipping Campden is one of the loveliest medieval wool towns with many beautiful, honey coloured stone buildings. It reached the height of its prosperity in the 14th century. However by 1902 it had suffered a decline, and there were empty buildings for workshops and schools, cottages available to let, all in a picturesque, quasi-medieval setting. The journey from Mile End Road to Chipping Campden must have appeared to some of the men as a journey from the dawn of the 20th century back in time. The picturesque stone buildings and the air of semi-dereliction fitted the Guild's own mythology of a revival of lost medieval England.

So with the Guildsmen's families, the group was around one hundred and fifty and the influx gave the town a much needed fresh injection of life. The investment by the Guild was significant. It acquired a lease on the Old Silk Mill as its headquarters and main studio facility, and renamed it Essex House. They also took a number of empty and derelict cottages for the craftsmen and their families. The School of Handicraft, which had been established in London, moved into a large, disused malt house in the grounds of Elm Tree House alongside Ashbee's architects office. Other Guild buildings in the town included Braithwaite House, to provide accommodation for the younger, unattached craftsmen, and further space was found for the Guild Library and Museum. The impact on this sleepy Cotswold town, through the number of people and buildings occupied, and the challenge to established ways of life, was profound.

A place of his abiding affection: the High Street, Chipping Campden, a pen and ink drawing by JHB in 1939.

The move to these Elysian Fields, although romantic, was to prove commercially challenging. The output of the craftsmen was either commissioned or sold in high-class London stores to a wealthy middle-class market, who appreciated hand-made products. Although the Guild produced some of its best work during this period, they struggled financially and in the autumn of 1907 the Guild of Handicraft Limited went into liquidation. Ashbee was an idealist not a businessman, and the move had increased the distance between the craftsmen and their London customers. There was also a national slump in trade and increasing competition from cheaper products, which were in part machine-made in London and Birmingham.

Although it had failed as a commercial venture, the Guild had not failed as an innovative cultural and social movement. In 1909, the leading craftsmen formed a reconstituted organisation, the Guild of Handicraft Trust, which sustained the bond between them, although they were now all working independently. They also continued to run the School of Handicraft as an integral part of their activities. Significantly for JHB, they organised summer schools which he discovered on his bicycle ride in 1913 and he attended a further two in 1914 and 1915. During this time JHB completed his art school training and was a teaching assistant at the Leicester Art School, working towards his teaching qualification. The classes in Campden were taught by leading craftsmen and JHB initially studied silversmithing under George Hart, who was soon to play an important role in his life. He also studied carving in wood and stone, which before too long he was to develop as a career.

Some staff and students at the Guild of Handicraft Summer School in 1914. George Hart (1882-1973) is third from left, standing with thumbs under armpits, his characteristic pose. JHB is standing on the steps at the centre without a smock.

ARTISTS AND CRAFTSMEN OF INFLUENCE

The leading Guildsmen influenced JHB but so too did other key figures, a number of whom went on to become his great friends and mentors. Benjamin Fletcher, who was Head of the Leicester School during JHB's time, attended an early summer school in jewellery-making at Chipping Campden in 1903. There he met Sydney Reeve, a Guild silversmith, and persuaded him to come to work in Leicester where Reeve must have encouraged JHB in his craft. Fletcher is a major figure in the history of design education in the UK and would have been a strong presence when JHB was a student and later a teaching assistant. He pioneered a wide range of craft teaching in Leicester and developed strong links with local industry.

Due to his success, Fletcher moved to Birmingham in 1920 to become Head of the School of Art, and Director of Art Education for the city. JHB kept in regular touch with him and sometime later, Fletcher provided a glowing reference, illustrating a mutual respect and a sense of shared values.

A further link between Leicester and the Guild of Handicraft Trust was the Arts and Crafts architect and furniture designer, Ernest Gimson. He was Leicester-born and trained at the Leicester School of Art. He then joined a London architectural practice with strong links to William Morris where he met Ernest and Sidney Barnsley. They went on to form the Cotswold School, designing and making furniture not far from the Guild.

When he joined the summer school in 1913, JHB concentrated on silver work and made several fine pieces in the Arts and Crafts style. George Hart, the silversmith, was one of the leading Guildsmen and he was to be a seminal figure in JHB's life over the next few years. He was an outstanding craftsman who not only built an international reputation for his work, but created a dynasty of silversmiths who continue to work in the Old Silk Mill in Chipping Campden to this day.

The second major figure for JHB was the sculptor and carver, Alec Miller. He was also a leading Guildsman and the one most receptive to Ashbee's ideas. Like George Hart, he

Calf's Lane, Chipping Campden in 1917, a wood engraving by Fred Griggs (1876-1938).

continued to participate fully in sustaining the Guild of Handicaft and its School after the initial company failed. He was a mentor to JHB, became his employer, and a friend. It was through Miller that JHB first taught in Oxford. Miller was an outstanding craftsman, working mostly from commissions including carved portraits from wood, one of the most difficult craft skills.

Another significant figure was Fred Griggs who came to Campden in 1903 to illustrate a travel book and stayed for the rest of his life. He was never a member of the Guild but many of his close friends were Guild craftsmen. He was a distinguished etcher, architectural draughtsman, illustrator and early conservationist, one of the first etchers to be elected as a full member of the Royal Academy. It was his drawing style that influenced JHB. He and Griggs both became entranced by the honey coloured stone buildings that Griggs did so much to preserve. It is easy to see Griggs' influence on JHB's drawing style.

There were many eminent visitors to the Guild too, including the artist Walter Crane, the ceramicist William De Morgan, the socialists Sydney and Beatrice Webb, the author Laurence Houseman, the poet John Masefield, the painter Holman Hunt, and the designer and artist Eric Gill. Others who followed to the Cotswolds included the furniture designer and manufacturer Gordon Russell, the Winchcombe Pottery, and later the industrial designer Robert Welch.

During this time, JHB came into contact with May Morris, daughter of William Morris but also an established designer in her own right. She was the keeper of both her father's reputation and many of his artefacts. She remained living at her father's home, Kelmscott Manor in Oxfordshire, which JHB visited and where he would take students on pilgrimages in future years.

JHB also knew and corresponded with the pioneering design educationalist William Lethaby, the founder of the Central School of Arts and Crafts in 1896. In 1901 Lethaby was appointed the first Professor of Design at the Royal College of Art. He was the first to propose breaking down academic barriers between design, seen as an artistic and intellectual pursuit, and production, the less sophisticated activity of the craftsman. He suggested that they were both taught as equally valuable parts of the process of producing high-quality products.

EDUCATIONAL IDEALS

The Arts and Crafts Movement's influence was far and wide, and parallel movements developed in the United States and to some extent in Europe. Many of the Guild's own practices guided other ventures, like the Bauhaus, the German art and design school and movement of the 1920s. In Germany and in Austria, design was widely appreciated and was making a significant contribution to industry.

The Movement's ideals, promoting a simple life and a respect for land and nature, blossomed again in the 1960s and 1970s when self-sufficiency was of particular interest. Today, in the second decade of the 21st century, another craft revival is happening in various parts of the western world but particularly emerging around Silicon Valley, the high tech hub in California. Words like artisan, maker and provenance are surfacing again in vocabulary. While innovation heralds progress, the need to get back to simpler ways is, perhaps, a cyclical human desire not to feel too far removed from nature and to gain fulfilment by making things.

During his time at the Guild, JHB absorbed many of these ideas, and the wider interests and working philosophies of Ashbee and the more intellectual members of the Guild. JHB also witnessed opportunity and education for all - the Guild recruited men from all sorts of backgrounds and the School of Handicraft was an integral part of the Guild from the outset. There was also an interdependence between the Guild and the School: Guildsmen taught in order to pass on their skills, and pupils were absorbed into the Guild, putting into practice the revived medieval concept of apprenticeship.

Art and design training was carried out alongside production. Ashbee believed that architects should be knowledgeable about and work closely with building and builders. JHB was to later implement exactly this in Oxford and it reinforced his principal belief: that education should be close to the world of work.

But Guild life more broadly would also influence JHB's activities in his later years. Colleagues and families lived and worked closely together, another concept taken from an earlier age. They made music, put on plays and entertainment, and frequently ate together at suppers, often in combination with Guild lectures. Ashbee also liked the Greek idea of physical fitness being essential for a keen mind, so he supported athletic activities and sports, such as the Guild cricket team and many other activities. He said, *"Good craftsmanship springs from a good and healthy life."* He encouraged involvement in the governance of the Guild, believing that worker participation was important for society in general. He believed that a happy and fulfilled craftsman would produce better work.

WORLD WAR ONE

By 1914, British global influence was passing. During the 19th century, Britain had enjoyed unparalleled peace and prosperity, but the root of its success - industrialisation - was causing social problems at home. Nationalism was developing in Europe, and the economy and military power of Germany grew rapidly following the unification in 1871. There were significant challenges to British supremacy, and tensions evolved throughout Europe during the second decade of the 20th century.

As the pressure grew, many British citizens, particularly the new socialists and various religious groups, questioned Government policy. Among them were many of JHB's associates, some Guild members, teachers from Leicester and in particular his father, Robert Brookes. Robert, who was deeply religious and a committed pacifist, joined a group of like-minded teachers and some industrialists on a peace mission to Germany in May 1914. They had support from both governments and undertook an extensive tour including visiting Berlin. But the rifts in Europe continued and war was declared in August 1914.

The British Secretary of State for War, Lord Kitchener's Your Country Needs You campaign was very successful and volunteers joined up from across society. Britain had strong agricultural and manufacturing economies; when an owner's sons volunteered, it was expected that the workers would follow and they did. The country dwellers around Chipping Campden typified the enthusiasm for the war and they expected a rapid victory. JHB did not volunteer.

JHB's father, Robert Brookes, second from left, on a peace mission to Germany in May 1914 with a group of teachers and industrialists.

But the war did not proceed as expected. In the first two years the British death toll was huge and the forces were running out of troops. For the first time in history, conscription was enforced in 1916 when the Government passed the Military Service Act. JHB, no doubt greatly influenced by his father, some of his teaching colleagues, and some members of the Guild and their circle, registered as a conscientious objector.

It greatly affected his outlook and decisions in later life. He faced disapproval from some members of his family and many country people from the Campden area. Although conscientious objectors were much criticised at the time and many were ostracised, it was a brave decision based on his moral principles; almost a hundred years later, many in society would take a similar view. JHB rarely talked about his decision but he did reflect on it in a letter to Alec Miller years later in 1957 as *"an uneasy period in which I attempted to square my own conscience and to help [local people]."*

By 1916 George Hart, who was an experienced farmer, was living at Holly Bush Farm at nearby Broad Campden with his wife Edith, and continuing his craft as a silversmith. Ashbee had persuaded American millionaire Joseph Fels to buy the seventy-acre farm in 1908 so that the Guildsmen of the emerging Guild of Handicraft Trust could be self-sufficient. Farming was a reserved occupation so Hart, who had served in the Boer War, was exempt from military service. He offered JHB the chance to work on the farm for the remaining war years. Although from an urban background, JHB had fallen in love with the Cotswold countryside, so the farm and the practical work he so revered suited him:

> *"…not only was George an exceptionally fine silversmith but a very efficient farmer, too. Some time later an invitation to live in at the farm proved irresistible. Once installed it was difficult to know whether one's main role was that of a deplorably inadequate young silversmith or that of a shockingly awkward farm labourer, or exactly when on or off duty. This might depend partly on the season or partly on the job in hand. I was devastating with a hoe in the potato field or up and down our few acres of swedes, and the farm's gate posts were in real danger when I was in charge of our spirited two-horse team. But in time I attained a somewhat modest proficiency with the small milking herd and at rearing motherless lambs which soon became the most faithful and the most inconvenient of pets."*

One of JHB's tasks was to milk the cows and then deliver the milk, which required a 5.30am start each day, a habit that remained with him for the rest of his life. Through the war years, JHB, known by his family name 'Jack', also continued his teaching interests when time permitted, teaching in local schools, to church groups and in village halls.

'JACK' THE COTSWOLD CRAFTSMAN

The tragedies and horrors of the war ended with an armistice on 11 November 1918. Alec Miller had been exempted from military service through being medically unfit with curvature of the spine. Along with a number of other craftsmen, he lived and worked in Chipping Campden through the war years, though there was barely enough work to scrape a living. When trade improved in 1919, Alec Miller offered JHB a job as studio assistant. JHB had a keen interest in lettering and would soon become proficient in carving under Miller's tutelage.

Many of the studio's commissions were war memorials, often of stone or simple wood tablets. It was no doubt rather poignant work for them both. Most of these memorials were installed in Gloucestershire and Oxfordshire, and a few were designed by Fred Griggs. A major commission was for Coventry Cathedral. The statue was the largest single piece Miller ever undertook. JHB worked on it too, probably carving the lettering. The whole work was destroyed in a 1940 air raid on Coventry in World War Two.

Alec Miller (1879-1961) with a statue of St Michael, carved for Coventry Cathedral in 1922. JHB worked with him on a range of carvings for the Cathedral. All were destroyed during the air raids of World War Two.

The Cotswolds also brought JHB his wife. Whilst working on the farm, he met Helena Victoria Mary Tyack, known as Lena. She was the daughter of a Worcestershire market gardener and innkeeper, and was in Chipping Campden working for an aunt as a housekeeper. They married in her home village of Harvington, Worcestershire on 7 October 1919 and moved into a small cottage in Cider Lane, Chipping Campden. They soon moved on to a more comfortable home at Elm Bank Cottage in Broad Campden, and although far from wealthy, settled happily into a Cotswold village life:

> *"I still marvel at the good fortune which permitted me to work in Chipping Campden for some eight years. Although so many have sung the praises of the former, few will have heard of Broad Campden, a modest hamlet of thirty or forty houses, most of which are not even visible from the narrow road which winds towards Draycott and Blockley. We called our cottage 'Elm Bank' for it topped a steep grassy mound which had in its centre the hollow trunk of an ancient elm. A rough footpath straggled up the bank and by the door and led to a disused Friends' meeting house, fading out at a stile, beyond which*

was a pleasant meadow. A second footpath on the far side of the bank passed between the small church and a cottage which served as a village inn."

On 30 September 1920, a daughter, Joan, was born and on 2 February 1923 a son, Peter, followed. The family successfully integrated into Guild and village life, with JHB joining in theatrical events and giving talks at village halls.

Alec Miller was widely acknowledged as an extremely able sculptor, with work at the Royal Academy throughout the 1920s and many exhibitions. But in a difficult economy, the commercial life of the studio was precarious. Miller supplemented his income by teaching and lecturing; among his contacts were Oxford-based architects and stonemasons, and the Oxford School of Art.

Although he may have undertaken lettering work around Oxford, it was in 1922 that JHB really became involved with Oxford when he stepped in for Alec Miller who couldn't fulfil teaching engagements. JHB met some of the Oxford stonemasons and taught at the Oxford School of Art. He also met the architect Thomas Rayson, who had commissioned carvings from Miller for various Oxford buildings. Another key Oxford personality of these years was Basil Blackwell, son of the founder of the well-known Oxford bookseller, who was a good friend of Miller and who would become a staunch friend and supporter of JHB.

When the Head of the Oxford School of Art, Francis Wood, was taken ill and needed a prolonged absence in 1923/4, JHB applied for the temporary post with Miller's blessing. The governors engaged him and he clearly did an outstanding job. A colleague at that time, Arthur Flemming, the Headmaster of the Municipal Secondary School that was housed in the same building, summed up:

"...I have formed the highest possible opinion of Mr Brookes as a teacher. Teaching is as much a matter of personality as of technique and Mr Brookes is gifted with a personality which can establish in a very short time, a mutual and warm sympathy between him and his students...it is this as much as his skill as an artist and a craftsman which makes his teaching so effective."

During this period, JHB was able to finish his teaching qualification, which had been interrupted by the war, getting his Art Teacher's Diploma in 1923. Although not a university graduate, the qualification gave him graduate status for salary purposes.

With his natural abilities, JHB could have pursued a career as an artist/craftsman or a teacher. He loved his work as a craftsman in the idyllic setting of the Cotswolds:

"At the end of a day's work at the bench there was always some fresh delight: an evening stroll to Norman Chapel, Charles Ashbee's wonderful house at Broad Campden, with good conversation followed by Mrs Ashbee's delightful playing on the harpsichord: or evening walks to Blockley, Broadway, Willersey, or Saintbury; a midnight picnic on Dovers Hill: an impromptu sketch club at Alec Miller's studio."

The Brookes and Miller families became close, and both Miller and JHB made delightful carvings of the young Joan Brookes. But the studio struggled financially and Miller decided to explore wider opportunities. He made his first visit to the United States in 1924 and found that there was a ready market for his work. He held one-man shows, gave a number of lectures and gained portrait commissions from wealthy individuals. After many years working for church bodies, he stated with some feeling how he longed for some really "pagan work" to do.

For a while Alec Miller had worked in partnership with Will Hart, who in the early days of the Guild had been Miller's assistant and was brother of George Hart, the silversmith who had supported JHB in the war years. Will Hart's career was divided between military service and Guild craftsmanship. He had served both in the Navy and the Army, and enlisted in 1915, becoming a major. He relinquished his service in 1920 and returned to Chipping Campden. Perhaps he was jealous of the bond between Miller and his new assistant JHB, as it seems that Will Hart was one of the few men with whom JHB did not get along. A letter from Will Hart to Ashbee in February 1923 captures the sentiment:

> *"I fought in the Great War to assist in preserving if possible the great traditions of our empire of which we ought to be greatly proud! In Campden even, we have the underminers at work, eg Brookes and his like, who are not ready to defend their country but would countenance the spilling of blood to wreck if possible our National traditions."*

Alec Miller's interests in the United States increased. A fellow Guild assistant, Edgar Keene, tried to emigrate to the United States in 1923 only to be turned back at Ellis Island because the quota was full.

With the unpredictable flow of work at the studio and a family to support, JHB seems to have been unsettled. In mid-1924, JHB decided to seek more secure employment and successfully applied for the job of Art Master at Penistone Grammar School, near Sheffield in Yorkshire.

THE TEACHER EMERGES

The move to Yorkshire was a significant change for JHB and his young family. Joan recalls moving into a little house on a steep hill below the church, leaving their beloved Cotswolds with heavy hearts. JHB, now aged 33, started work in 1924 and tackled the job with his usual enthusiasm.

Whilst in Yorkshire JHB continued his own education by attending classes and also supplemented his experience and income by teaching history of art and architecture at the extra-mural department of Sheffield University. Headmaster of Penistone, G W Morris, was appreciative:

> *"Mr Brookes, as his record makes clear, is artist and craftsman both in wood and metal; this variety of experience gives him a width of outlook invaluable in an Art teacher. Under his direction... all the pupils in the two forms that sit for the Northern Universities Matriculation Examination offer Art, including the History of Architecture, as a matriculation subject; from all the candidates rarely more than one or two fail. His lectures on the History of Art and on Craftwork are most effective.*
>
> *"From the administrative point of view Mr Brookes is methodical, prompt and businesslike. His relations with colleagues and pupils are of the happiest; he is always ready to lend a hand in an emergency or to help with the organisation of School functions."*

These words were written by Morris in a reference for JHB in the spring of 1928. It is probable that the architect Thomas Rayson, who did some teaching at the Oxford School of Art, told JHB of the advertisement for a Head of the School on the retirement of Mr Wood. JHB, knowing the school from his earlier experience and probably wanting to be closer to both Helena's and his family plus Cotswold friends, applied for the job. He was successful.

Left: Helena Brookes (1897-1980) photographed about 1919, the time of her marriage to JHB.

Below: A pencil drawing of daughter Joan when 17 months old in February 1922. It is from a sketch book JHB made to record his children's early years.

A JHB drawing of Church Street, St Ebbe's with the School's main entrance in the centre, c1940s.

JHB was by any measure an excellent choice: a man who had appropriate experience and attitudes for the challenge of building further education in Oxford. He was an accomplished artist, craftsman and designer; an experienced teacher having shown insight and ability to inspire others; and he had proven his potential for leadership and administrative capabilities.

So in 1928, aged 37, JHB was appointed Head of the Oxford School of Art and Vice-Principal of the Oxford City Technical School. It was a grand title but a small institution: the School of Art at that time had two full-time staff and 90 students, mostly taught in the evenings.

The influence of his teacher father, his years in Leicester and at the Guild, and his close friendships, had all allowed him to develop his educational ideas. These ideas would guide him as he took up his appointment in Oxford. His personal strengths, ability to inspire others and prodigious work ethic, were all about to be tested.

THE EDUCATOR
1928 – 1945

Previous page: Some of the staff of the Oxford Schools of Technology, Art and Commerce with JHB in the centre front row and Arnold Wainwright, Head of the Junior Technical School, on his right in St Ebbe's in the mid-1940s.

Below: The Taylor Institution on St Giles, Oxford c1900.

THE EDUCATOR
1928 – 1945

The task that JHB faced when he arrived in Oxford in 1928 would have daunted many. Housed in modest buildings of a dozen rooms were a secondary school, a junior art school, technical evening classes, a small full-time art school as well as Saturday classes for pupil teachers. This inadequate provision had been the story of the Oxford School of Art right from the beginning in 1865.

The School was founded and supported by a visionary group of local notables. They included Dr Henry Liddell, Dean of Christ Church and sometime Vice-Chancellor of the University of Oxford, and father of Alice Liddell, who inspired the heroine of Lewis Carroll's Alice in Wonderland; Sir Henry Acland, the eminent medical scholar; Frederick Morrell, solicitor to the University and member of the Oxford brewing family; and The Duke of Marlborough. These gentlemen made subscriptions to finance the School and its students. It was a philanthropic act, no doubt prompted by a social attitude that some educational provision should be made for the working classes. The first class took place on 22 May 1865, in a room probably on the ground floor of the Taylor Institution on St Giles' in Oxford, lent free by the curators.

Although Britain was the first industrialised nation and acknowledged as the workshop of the world, the Industrial Revolution highlighted the inadequacies of the education system. Britain's colonial empire and its economy grew during the 19th century, but its industrial decline was identified following the Great Exhibitions of 1851 in London and 1867 in Paris. Public opinion was aroused when it became evident that output from France, Germany and the USA would soon challenge Britain's supremacy. As a result, the Department of Practical Art was set up, becoming the Department of Science and Art in 1853. Known as the Kensington system, the result was financial support to schools and organised exams in areas relevant to industry.

However, Oxford's economy was, and had been for many years, mainly dependent on the University of Oxford. The overriding culture was one of educational elitism: providing a classical education pursuing knowledge for its own sake, eschewing anything practical.

The consequences of this for technical teaching are perhaps an example of the town-gown social divide in the city. When compared to the industrial towns and cities of the North, Midlands and London, Oxford was late in starting art and technical teaching, and was some six years after Cambridge. Oxford's applied education began through a few farsighted individuals who foresaw the social and economic implications of an industrial society. The Oxford School of Art was an immediate success with 126 enrolments in the first year, more than doubling in year two. Rather than create a separate school of science, it broadened into science teaching, becoming the School of Science and Art in 1870. Science classes were held in the University Museum, now the Natural History Museum, whilst the art classes had moved to a room in the Randolph Galleries, now part of the Ashmolean Museum. The science subjects that were offered included mathematics, magnetism and electricity, animal physiology and inorganic chemistry; all classes were taught in the evenings.

In 1872, university committee minutes give an insight into the prevailing social attitudes to applied learning and educating the 'artizan classes'. They record that Professor John Ruskin endowed a School of Drawing at the University of Oxford for the 'upper and middle classes'. The consequences were a step backwards for the School of Art, which was educating the 'artizan' and working classes; it was compelled to leave its accommodation for a much smaller space in the basement, and some teaching was lost. But while art teaching struggled, science flourished with the help of facilities loaned by the University and Oxford colleges, and with some help from the City of Oxford Education Committee.

During the 1880s, increased industrial competition at last spurred the development of technical education in Britain. In London, the livery companies founded the City and Guilds of London Institute, which established national standards in technical, craft and trade subjects, and a number of art and technical institutions were established. Various commissions reported and associations were formed, culminating in the Technical Instruction Act of 1889, which allowed local councils to support technical instruction. In Oxford, this would bring to an end the dedicated voluntary body who for twenty-five years had struggled to provide the only teaching that was available to the working classes of the city. When Oxford City Council took over the management of the School in 1891, the institution was renamed the 'Oxford City Technical School' and it incorporated the School of Art.

In 1894, under council management, Oxford City Technical School moved to its own premises in Church Street, St Ebbe's. The building had been an old Bluecoat School, founded on a charitable basis in 1710, and its two rooms were modestly expanded at a cost of £3,000. The School's student numbers grew rapidly, and the premises became so inadequate for teaching that the government grant was withdrawn in 1900.

The School's existence was only saved by the Education Act 1902, which created local education authorities with some funding for technical education. With this increased national interest in educating the population in art and technical skills, the Oxford City Technical School should have been on a more solid footing, but resource was tight. The local authority in Oxford could have raised additional funding within the city during the early years of the 20th century. After all, industry was developing, needing an increasingly equipped workforce. William Morris, who shared the same name as the founder of the Arts and Crafts Movement, had started building cars. This William Morris, later Lord Nuffield, had studied engineering at the Technical School, probably through part-time evening teaching. Technical education in the more industrialised towns and cities continued to flourish, but Oxford's economy was still largely dependent on the University and the culture was slow to change. So the Technical School was not given increased funding. When JHB took up his post in 1928, the need for determination and vision were all too apparent.

A DIFFICULT INHERITANCE: INADEQUATE PREMISES

With so many students being taught in such inadequate premises, JHB noted: *"I quickly learned the need for constant improvisation... an ability to share the oddest of odd corners with apparent strangers."*

A JHB scraper-board of an overhead view of the Church Street premises with surrounding buildings in St Ebbe's, Oxford c1940s.

The buildings in Church Street, St Ebbe's, were richly described in the memories of a member of staff, arriving for an interview:

> *"...an old building which was such a queer mixture of styles - part pseudo-gothic with stone mullion windows, part hideous red-brick (and with a wooden hut of World War One thrown in) - that it resembled a junk yard. The entrance was through two enormous dark green doors which opened onto a cobbled way. On passing through these doors, the visitor appeared to be in a mad coal-merchant's yard where heaps of coke had been tipped haphazardly. At the sight of all this I almost turned and fled.*
>
> *"Threading my way among heaps of coke and piles of bicycles, I made my way to a tumble down building in the corner of the yard. The outside appearance was utterly dismal but on entering, I was greeted with the warmest of welcomes...After some*

friendly conversation (and a cheering cup of tea), both of which brightened my gloom, I was taken to the Principal's room and met Mr J H Brookes. A pleasant half hour with him convinced me that human warmth was of far greater importance than depressing buildings."

Without doubt, this warmth must have been a crucial ingredient in the success and achievements of the next thirty years. The premises were so dire that it must have taken a good deal of JHB's personal persuasion to support his staff and to develop his new ideas in the face of seemingly insurmountable hurdles.

JHB later discovered that a longstanding battle between the local authority and the then Board of Education continued to rage over the inadequacy of the premises.

IMMEDIATE PROGRESS

JHB was quick out of the starting blocks. He was well-prepared for the post through his training and experience at Leicester, at the Guild in Chipping Campden, and his earlier experience of teaching in Yorkshire and Oxford. He was also fully aware how technical education had developed more extensively in other cities.

Following his appointment but before he arrived in Oxford, JHB was planning two new areas of study for the School and was working on the recruitment of suitable teachers.

The first was the revival of printing instruction, which had taken place as evening classes before the outbreak of war in 1914. Although he did not take up his appointment until September 1928, he met with the formidable Dr John Johnson, Printer to the University, in effect the Head of Oxford University Press and Mr A C Cameron, the Secretary of the City of Oxford Education Committee, to make plans.

Reading about it now, it almost seems like an act of magic. His predecessor had tried to form printing classes with and for Dr Johnson but had failed. JHB had a similar paucity of space and teaching resource, but with his warm manner, persuasive approach and steely determination, he formed a strong relationship with Dr Johnson, who was also keen to make progress as he had only recently been appointed in 1925. Printing instruction was set up in both the limited space of the School and in generously donated accommodation at the University Press. JHB somehow persuaded Johnson to provide space, equipment, even teachers and most of the students, but then still to claim the activity for the School of Art.

Johnson's assistant, Charles Batey, worked closely with JHB to set up courses on composition, typography and book binding. This was the beginning of the Printing School, which JHB felt was one of his greatest achievements. Batey, who would take over as University Printer in 1946, wrote:

"Here was revealed his quick appreciation of a situation requiring immediate action: here was resolution and enterprise: here was courage. For he had no materials, no teachers and no premises. But he had much faith; and charged as he was with the still confidence which has remained such a large part of him, he went forward."

The second area of study that JHB initiated was architecture. Like printing, architecture was a long established profession in Oxford, serving the University's needs. Indeed Oxford had hosted some nationally recognised architects, such as George Edmund Street, a leading revivalist of Gothic architecture, who worked in Oxford in the 1850s and was later associated with Philip Webb, and the young artist/craftsman William Morris.

A JHB pen and ink drawing of his family home at the Gate House, 195 The Slade, Headington built in 1929, drawn in 1973.

When JHB arrived, there were evening classes in building construction but not architecture. However his friend, the architect Thomas Rayson, who did some teaching at the Oxford School of Art, had seen a local need to train young architects. He delivered basic teaching both at his office and on Sunday afternoons at his home in Jericho for his own pupils and those from other offices. Out of Rayson's enthusiasm, and perhaps a sense of deprivation, these pupils formed their own club, the Doric Club in 1927, which is still going strong today. It was the enthusiastic young members of the Doric Club, including two recently established Oxford architects Ronald Fielding Dodd and Thomas Lawrence Dale who, with Thomas Rayson, approached the newly-appointed JHB with the idea of starting a School of Architecture. JHB of course saw the opportunity and agreed to set up a course but as with printing, there was no staff, no money and no space.

The first course, the foundations of the School of Architecture, began as an enormous act of faith in September 1929. Fielding Dodd agreed to teach a course and offered an attic room above his studio in Turl Street. JHB persuaded the City of Oxford Education Committee to support the plan and during that year a full-time teacher, Mr S N Bertram, a qualified architect, was appointed. The School was beginning its journey of rapid growth.

Both printing and architecture grew from the close associations that JHB maintained with employers and businesses in Oxford. The sustained support these employers gave to the Technical School and to JHB was to be essential for the School's development, but this close working was also at the heart of JHB's educational philosophy.

JHB knew that he had to make an impact on Oxford more widely. He also needed to discover and foster the interest of key individuals within the University of Oxford, involve more local business people and develop support from councillors. He quickly proved to be very adept at public relations: he wrote well and was an engaging speaker. He saw the value of public events, arranging for annual meetings and prize-giving events to be at the Town Hall or other public buildings in Oxford. He invited as many local worthies as he could muster and made sure that representatives of the press were in attendance. From the outset of his time in Oxford, he carefully filed press cuttings in a series of books; he knew the power of communications of all sorts.

Somehow he also found time to commission his friend Thomas Rayson to design the Gate House, 195 The Slade, Headington, and the family moved there in 1929. It was a fine detached house on the edge of Oxford, facing rural Wood Farm in the foothills of Shotover. It was to be the family home for the rest of his life, now marked with a Blue Plaque.

JHB enjoyed a warm and close family life. As in many things his father was a role model: highly moral, hard-working and technically capable. JHB's early family life was loving and close knit and he sustained a strong, respectful relationship with both his parents. JHB cared deeply about his sister Margaret, who like most of her family, spent a career in education. She ran a small school in Skipton, Yorkshire. JHB was keen to support his sister and on coming to Oxford in 1928, sent his eight year-old daughter, Joan, to board in Yorkshire with her aunt. Joan, direct and modest as her father, said *"I was treated just the same as the other children."*

JHB, although always focused on his career, was a more modern father than many of his era. In a sketch book, he made beautiful portraits of his wife and the children through their early years, and he also recorded the children's weights over their first six months.

Both Joan and Peter were academically bright children and they went to secondary school in Oxford, Joan to Milham Ford and Peter to Magdalen College School. Joan was always closer to her father and Peter to his mother. The family roles of JHB and his wife, Helena, were of their time: JHB was the bread winner and Helena was the housewife. They appear to have established their roles from the outset and to have led a happy married life.

OXFORD MAIL, THURSDAY, 23

OXFORD ART STUDENTS' SUCCESS

A press cutting from *Oxford Mail* in July 1931 showing JHB with students.

LIFTING THE BAR: INVALUABLE CONNECTIONS

Regardless of the working conditions, JHB knew that one way of motivating students was to invite leading figures of the day to the School. He had learned from similar memorable experiences at Leicester and when at the Guild of Handicraft. Amongst those he invited were Sir Clough Williams-Ellis, a well-known architect of the interwar years, who is best known as creator of the Italianate village of Portmeirion in North Wales. Williams-Ellis was an idiosyncratic character who no doubt inspired the students. JHB sustained a lifelong friendship with the eminent architect and in later life made drawings of Williams-Ellis's work at Cornwell, near Chipping Norton.

Another visitor was Noel Carrington, an outstanding book designer, who was one of the most influential figures of the 20th century in the design, commissioning and editing of children's books. He was the originator of Puffin Books and later worked for Oxford University Press. His sister was Dora Carrington, the artist and well known member of the Bloomsbury Group. A third visitor from this time was art historian, Kenneth Clarke, later Lord Clarke, who in 1969 produced and presented the popular BBC series 'Civilisation'. He was a proponent of modern art, particularly abstract expressionism. Alec Miller didn't like this emerging style of art and so the same is probably true of JHB, who had been guided by Miller in the arts and crafts tradition.

These visitors are testament to JHB's determination to give his students the best opportunities and to his persuasive powers in attracting such internationally well-known figures to his humble premises. Even though he may not have agreed with their ideas or enthusiasms, he thought it right that his students should hear different opinions, an open-mindedness that must have created memorable moments for the School's students.

JHB fully realised the social and economic influence of the University of Oxford. Three senior figures would prove to be great supporters and wise advisors to him and the School. Sir Michael Sadler was one of the early supporters. He was the Master of University College, an historian, educationalist and owner of a remarkable collection of expressionist art, including works by Wassily Kandinsky and Paul Gauguin. As well as his active support to JHB, he regularly lent pieces from his superb collection for the students to study. It might be a painting, a sculpture or a piece of silver with a little note informing the students about them. This fortnightly session he called 'Brookes Pulpit'. Interestingly he was approached in the late 1920s to promote the idea of creating an architecture course at the University of Oxford. However he dismissed the idea believing it would be better placed under JHB's direction.

Another major supporter from the University was Sir Kenneth Wheare, an Australian academic, expert on constitutional history, Gladstone Professor of Government, Rector of Exeter College and later in his career, Vice-Chancellor of the University. He was a university member of the City Council and later became Chairman of the City Education Committee and the chair of governors. He seems a kindred spirit to JHB and is quoted as saying, *"Over my dead body, if I may take up a moderate position in this matter."*

The support of University Printer Dr John Johnson, through his work with JHB on printing teaching, would prove invaluable in wider Oxford circles too. He was hugely influential in the city holding a senior role in the University and as the leader of a substantial workforce at Oxford University Press. He would become a prominent Governor of the School.

At various times over three decades, these distinguished members of the University gave

Far left: A portrait of the architect Sir Clough Williams-Ellis (1883-1978) at Portmerion taken by John Hedgecoe in 1969.

Left: A portrait in oils of Sir Kenneth Wheare (1907-1979) by William Edward Narraway 1971.

great support to JHB, and rallied round the Secretary of the Oxford Education Committee to influence public opinion. This group seems to have a common bond; all were down to earth, forward thinkers who were not afraid to get involved and help change the status quo. It is a great insight into the educational ambitions of JHB that such men were attracted to his ideas and pursued his friendship.

JHB set out his educational philosophies from the start. In his first annual report he stated that architecture and building should be studied together, as he had seen working successfully at Leicester School and in Charles Ashbee's Chipping Campden practice. He believed that aesthetic and artistic studies should relate strongly to practical and technical teaching. In the second annual report, he set out his belief that vocational study is not in contradiction to academic work, and that teaching both produces a well-rounded student. However, not everyone agreed with JHB's educational views and policies. To many, they were radical ideas. Some employers, trade unionists and students in the building industry were concerned when teaching moved from the technical side of the School to the newly formed School of Architecture in the School of Art. The city's education leaders were apprehensive but JHB held his nerve and as time went by, his policies proved to have huge merit.

Throughout this period JHB also strove to improve standards wherever he could; for him lifting the bar was an essential role of leadership. Despite the dismal working conditions, he recruited staff of the highest calibre that he could attract and as the modest institution's reputation grew, students arrived from further afield including nearby counties, a few from European countries and even the United States.

One was a young Spanish student, Pablo Palazuelo, who studied architecture and building from 1933 to 1936. He won the School Prize in 1935 for the best student of the year. His great skill was draughtsmanship and rendering but he was to develop into the most famous artist to have studied at the School. His success as a painter followed his move to Paris in 1948 where he worked for twenty years building an international reputation as one of the most important abstract painters of his generation. No doubt JHB taught him; he would not have promoted abstract art but in his open-minded way would not have discouraged a young person in their interests either.

In the first few years, JHB taught for at least thirty-six hours a week, both day and evening classes. Although he had little choice with such limited resources, he also knew from his experience at the Guild of Handicraft that exchanges between the older, experienced craftsmen and their young students were important. He taught the new printing and architecture students, plus the art students in drawing, layout, lettering, sculpture, carving, and art and architecture appreciation. JHB seems to have always retained a generous spirit in teaching the next generation. Even though he also had significant administrative responsibilities as Head of the School, his commitment was indefatigable.

JHB understood the value of social activities too, and how they helped to strengthen the skills of students and create a common bond. He arranged a variety of social events, including those for the recently formed Doric Club for architecture students, alumni and staff, and created travel opportunities for students, including camping weekends in the Cotswolds and cruises abroad, including Scandinavia and the Mediterranean. He continually sought ways to open young eyes to new opportunities.

A perhaps surprising interest of JHB's, given his modest demeanour, was acting. He had witnessed the value of acting in Chipping Campden. Persuading colleagues and students to get to their feet and perform gave them confidence and valuable communication skills, so JHB formed the Oxford Art School Players and occasionally took a leading role himself. A performance of which he was particularly proud was *And so to Bed*, a comedy about Samuel Pepys, staged at the Oxford Playhouse in 1935 in its early location on Woodstock Road. JHB took the lead part of Pepys with members of staff, students and even Joan, his fifteen year-old daughter, taking roles.

During the early 1930s, JHB was perpetually frustrated by the lack of resource. In 1932 and again in 1937 it appears that he either applied for a Principalship in Essex or was perhaps approached. He certainly didn't lack ambition and no doubt his reputation was growing. There were huge challenges in Oxford but perhaps the sheer scale of the task bolstered his determination to stay and fulfil his vision.

ART AND TECHNOLOGY MERGE

1934 was a watershed year. By this time, there were over 200 students attending day classes and over 1,000 attending in the evenings. A series of events heralded new opportunities for JHB, and were essentially the foundation of much of the education in Oxford today.

First was the creation of Southfield School, now Oxford Spires Academy, which meant that some 170 grammar school boys moved from St Ebbe's to a new building to the east of the city. For a time, this eased a situation that had become almost desperate. It liberated space for courses being taught in borrowed premises and provided the opportunity to launch new ones.

Second, this enabled the full merger of the Oxford City Technical School and the Oxford School of Arts and Crafts, and JHB was appointed the new Principal of the new Oxford Schools of Technology, Art and Commerce.

Left: Pablo Palazuelo (1916-2007) in his studio in Madrid taken by his brother Enrique Palazuelo in 1970.

Below: A photograph of the cast of *And so to Bed* acted by the Oxford Art School Players. JHB, playing the lead role of Samuel Pepys is on the far right.

A cutting from the Oxford press in November 1936, noting the successful expansion of the Oxford Schools following JHB's appointment as Principal.

OXFORD SCHOOLS' RAPID EXPANSION.

TECHNOLOGY, ART AND COMMERCE.

NUMBER OF STUDENTS MORE THAN TREBLED IN TWO YEARS.

JHB believed that these three areas of applied learning should be developed together, and quickly seized this opportunity. Technical classes, which had mostly been taught in the evenings, could now be fully integrated, and commercial classes could be developed. The working relationship between architecture and building was formalised into one department, and courses in science and engineering were now developed.

Complementing the creation of Southfield School, JHB exercised his belief in secondary technical education by forming a new Junior Technical School, which twenty years later was to become Cheney School.

OXFORD HONOUR

In 1935, after seven years in Oxford, JHB, age 44, was awarded an Honorary Master of Arts degree by the University of Oxford. This was recognition indeed from an institution that not many years earlier saw little need for any applied learning in the city or to educate the working classes. The University Public Orator, Dr Cyril Bailey, captured JHB's achievement:

> *"Behold the high priest of the three Graces, Technology, Art and Commerce; which one of these is more important to the life of the community than another it is by no means easy to state. In temples as yet, scattered and of little charm he admits the young Oxonians to these mysteries. Is this to be wondered at, since he himself while yet a young student at Leicester won honour in both Arts and Crafts.*
>
> *Appointed seven years ago in charge of our Schools he has enormously increased the number of pupils and greatly enlarged their curriculum. For he has gathered together both architects, carpenters, printers and teachers to teach these students almost anything they might wish to learn. Now into his hands has been entrusted the whole of the education of the adolescents in this City of Oxford who wish to continue their training where they left off and to widen their outlook. Today he exerts his influence over nearly 2,000 students, infecting them with his own keenness and vigour.*
>
> *Such a man, of such energy, so devoted to the service of the public, surely ought to be enrolled in our own ranks; therefore I present to you Ioanes Henricus Brookes, Principal of these Schools, in order that he may be admitted to the dignity of Magister in artibus honoris causa."*

Perhaps infused with increased confidence, JHB set about organising new courses and finding a new site. In the next few years, new staff were recruited for the Junior Technical School, and the School of Architecture became recognised by the Royal Institute of British Architects (RIBA) which meant that the School's pupils were exempted the Intermediate RIBA exams. In the School of Technology, a full-time sandwich course in mechanical engineering started with almost forty students, and the engineering department gained approval for Higher National Diplomas and Certificates.

This growth in engineering in the late 1930s enabled the governors to increase the pressure on the City Education Committee and the Board of Education to find new premises. The changing economic climate, the effect of Lord Nuffield's Cowley factory, and the outstanding work of JHB had all played their part. The University of Oxford's attitude was also shifting, perhaps through the influence of Sadler, Wheare and others. A new two-and-a-half-acre site was found on the Cowley Road and work started immediately. In less than a year some of the site was equipped and in full use, with further plans and funds approved for moving the whole institution. However, the development was abruptly stopped when war was declared in September 1939.

OXFORD MAIL, SATURDAY, 9 MARCH, 1940

ON THE HOME FRONT : SCHOOLBOY

BOYS OF COWLEY ST. JOHN SCHOOL at work on the site of the proposed new municipal college in Cowley-road. The ground is being developed for allotments. The main part of the proposed building will not be constructed until after the war.

A press cutting from *Oxford Mail*, March 1940 showing a typical scene of the war period, 'Digging for Victory'.

THE WAR EFFORT

The School needed to respond to the national demands of wartime. Initially student numbers fell as young people were recruited to the military but they then increased quite quickly, filling new courses that supported the war effort. JHB wrote:

> *"with buildings in the City requisitioned and with many Oxford schools working double shifts in order to accommodate schools evacuated from danger areas, it seemed impossible either to house the ever increasing student load or to undertake new and specialised responsibilities expected of any technical school under war conditions."*

Courses were organised for women supervisors and engineering trainees, and in the evenings there was training in foremanship. It seems that local engineering firms could absorb all the trainees that could be taught and then ask for more.

Although priority was given to engineering subjects, there was an ever-growing demand for other courses. The country was in a state of siege so, as a way of sustaining morale, speakers were provided for servicemen in their camps and JHB re-organised teaching in art and technical subjects. Practical 'make do and mend' courses were set up to aid survival and hundreds of students attended courses in cookery, woodwork, tailoring and dressmaking, brickwork, keep fit and gardening to support the Dig for Victory campaign. Wartime production was underway on the premises too. Both at the new engineering facility at the Cowley Road site, and in St Ebbe's, lathes were installed to allow Sunday working and long evening shifts to make parts for the Pressed Steel Company.

As well as sustaining all these activities, in 1943 JHB became the Emergency Information Officer for the city, at the age of 53. He also undertook fire watching duties often accompanied by his daughter Joan; his son Peter joined the RAF. There is little to record how JHB, the conscientious objector from World War One, felt during these years. With his warmth, understanding of people and his diligent commitment to young people, he must have keenly sought out news and mourned the loss of life in the war years.

JHB, second left, showing the Lord Mayor of Oxford, Clement Bellamy, far right, the war-time manufacturing facilities at the Cowley Road site c1941.

REALISING THE VISION
1945 – 1956

Previous page: JHB photographed during the building of the new college at Headington with Gipsy Lane houses in the background in the 1950s. This photograph was the principal reference for Anthony Morris when painting the posthumous portrait of JHB, page 10.

REALISING THE VISION
1945 – 1956

By 1945, and perhaps even as early as 1928 when he first took on a leadership role in Oxford, JHB had very clear ideas about educating young people and a strong sense of purpose.

His ideas became a reality through the School's policies and were a fundamental part of the culture and approach of the institution. They show a profound understanding of human motivation and have a timeless quality to them.

First, he believed that education should be closely allied to the world of work and aimed to strengthen this throughout his leadership. He believed in education for livelihood, rather than the often quoted education for life, because he reflected that earning a living is the way of life for most people. He firmly believed that vocational learning was wholly compatible with an academic education for a well-rounded student.

Second, he had an overriding belief in young people and their potential. He supported the notion of apprenticeship: the young learning from the experienced, a medieval idea. JHB implemented this in the ways that were open to him, such as day and block release courses, pioneering sandwich courses, setting up advisory committees of practitioners and running teaching programmes in work places. He followed his great mentor, William Lethaby, who said *"All education should be apprenticeship and all apprenticeship should be education."*

Third, he believed that practical, technical skills were at the heart of an industrial economy. Combining technical know-how with design and creativity was the route to wealth creation and innovation, and he encouraged this fusion of capabilities. In the modern world this is the bedrock of successful national economies such as Germany and Japan, but this must have been a difficult path to travel in a city like Oxford in the 1940s.

He believed that business was one of the worthiest professions in which educated minds could be employed, producing wealth for the benefit of the community. He developed commercial and business training but lamented that during most of his career, business people did not recognise the value of business education and reciprocally most educationalists didn't recognise business management as a profession. He believed that a successful business required educated qualities such as a wide vision, discriminating judgement and intellectual self-confidence.

Fourth, JHB believed in educational opportunities for everyone, regardless of their starting point in life. He thought that education was the key to a fulfilled and happy life and to the creation of a civilised society. He had witnessed opportunities for all at the Guild of Handicraft where young men from poor and working class backgrounds had often started at the Guild School and then if capable, moved on to apprenticeships. He practised this policy when selecting students and in his active support of the youth and continuing education organisations in Oxford.

It seems likely that these ideas emerged from the powerful influences in his earlier life: the values instilled by his craftsman-teacher father, the writings of William Morris and the Arts and Crafts Movement, the practices of the Guild of Handicraft and its leading members, educational leaders such as William Lethaby and Benjamin Fletcher, and through close and regular observation of institutions in the more industrialised cities.

It also seems that JHB had great common sense. He was a man who faced the challenges and opportunities of life head on. A modest man, his tireless commitment to others seems to have often won him support. His management style was open and direct and although he never shied from expressing an opinion, he had generally thought through the issues beforehand. He must have chaired many initiatives, boards and committees, and it seems that he generally got his way. Reginald Grimshaw, who on leaving war service was appointed as the Head of the School of Art, knew him well:

> *"He had a talent for marking down who would be of most help to him in forwarding his aims and such was his transparent dedication to a cause that help was usually forthcoming. His staff work prior to an operation was truly remarkable and at a meeting where there might be controversy, one would find the majority already converted to his views, often repeating the very arguments he had used in previous discussions. It was fine if you were in agreement but disastrous if you were not: JHB's activities behind the scenes were truly efficient."*

Another colleague, Reginald Cave, Head of the School of Architecture, characterised JHB's personality:

> *"JHB was thirty seven when... he took on the somewhat daunting task in St Ebbe's, but Brookes was neither of a character nor a temperament to be daunted. Small in stature, he was great in all else; a realistic idealist with strongly held moral values, he had an intense sense of purpose and fun."*

A further attribute, part of marshalling an argument, was his careful administration and meticulous record keeping, evident in his personal and work files. He was a man blessed with almost perfect health and his Teacher's Service Book indicates that he had no time off for illness between 1925 and his retirement in 1956.

PREMISES CRISIS

The war acted as a catalyst for new thinking in national educational policy. The shortage of technical and scientific skills to support the war effort was a spur to producing the 1943 White Paper 'Educational Reconstruction', which advocated greater power to local education authorities to support further education. This was followed by the Percy Report on higher technological education in 1945, which outlined a new structure for technical education.

So the tide was turning nationally. In Oxford, the town-gown balance was changing too. The Nuffield Organisation had now become the major social and economic force in the area with many thousands employed at Cowley, and a plethora of smaller enterprises were springing up to support this large international business. The war had helped drive an even closer relationship between the Oxford Schools of Technology, Art and Commerce and local industry, which JHB as Principal was quick to nurture.

Towards the end of the war, JHB's frustration had been palpable but he always expressed it in a measured, constructive manner. In 1943 he wrote:

> *"... a new interest in technical and commercial education has developed throughout the country and that there is at last a consciousness that our existing provision is far from satisfactory..... if we are to hold our own in the competition for international markets which is sure to follow the peace, we must provide for industry and commerce, a new generation of technologists trained for the tasks which await them."*

A scraper-board by JHB of Church Street, St Ebbe's, Oxford showing the facade of the School's building; centre left, probably drawn in the early 1950s, appearing in *The Oxford Times* in 1959.

For over fifteen years, JHB had seen Oxford, with its reputation for knowledge and its growing population, poorly served in technical and vocational education. With no alternative teaching of any size in nearby towns, a wide region around Oxford was without decent provision as a result.

Most importantly, he had seen how the poor accommodation had led to missed opportunities for many young people and the consequent lack of trained, skilled technicians to serve Oxford's growing industrialisation. With the support of his governors, he relentlessly asked for support from the Local Education Authority and the Board of Education and constantly wrote letters and articles in the press, putting his case.

Following the end of the war, JHB was faced with the challenge of educating the huge number of returning war veterans with high expectations of a better life. The variety of classes increased rapidly as training for war production was replaced by resettlement schemes. Business training courses replaced courses for training engineers; the building industry was rekindled, demanding skilled craftsmen of all kinds; partly trained architects and other mature students, back from the Forces, sought the opportunity to qualify. Rehabilitation schemes were started for both men and women in a range of work, new apprentice training schemes were set up for day release and a new spirit of enthusiasm abounded. Although developing applied education for the young, working classes in Oxford still presented a raft of challenges, the new national thinking must have encouraged JHB.

To accommodate this influx of war returners, and without the planned new building, more teaching space was needed. Temporary facilities included a disused factory, a suite of rooms over a tradesman's garage, several church halls, a former Friends Meeting House, a social club and a vacated school for girls. The engineering workshops on the Cowley Road site were supplemented by a number of pre-fabricated huts for teaching building and domestic science subjects, along with a lecture room and some administrative space which JHB eventually moved into. The School of Architecture moved into the disused secondary girls' school, Milham Ford in Cowley Place, which is now part of St Hilda's College. The Department of Printing whose activities had mostly ceased during the war was resited in

A press cutting from *Oxford Mail* in 1950 showing photographs of the poor teaching conditions.

OXFORD MAIL, WEDNESDAY, DECEMBER 27, 1950

Grimmest of Oxford schools

Pupils of the Secondary Technical School, Oxford, which has classrooms in widely-separated streets, making one of their daily treks between lessons, and (right) part of the original fabric, dating back to the 1860s. These pictures, reproduced from the school magazine, "The Phoenix," indicate some of the difficulties under which the school works.

The entrance to the premises at 115, High Street—a dark passage. Classes, a canteen serving 180 meals a day, a hall for various events including occasional plays are here; and at all the premises evening classes are held.

Part of the playground and cycle accommodation.

rented premises in Juxon Street, Jericho, equipped with machinery lent and purchased. Despite its frugality, it attracted apprentices on day release from companies across the county.

Several papers and memos that JHB wrote to colleagues during this period capture the chronic state of affairs:

> *"...the present position beggars description, it is an intolerable burden."*
>
> *"In my fourteen years, nobody has been able to claim a room, a place or a desk of their own."*
>
> *"Students scarcely know the term elbow room."*

Reginald Grimshaw recorded his early impressions of the Church Street premises:

> *"...you had to beware splinters in the floor of the old First World War army hut at the back. Four Schools were based there Art, Commerce and Technology and the Junior Day School and the Heads shared a long, narrow room with a stone floor and a fixed bench down one long side. Naturally, as the last to come I had the bit where there was an uncontrollable drip from the skylight above during wet weather and a bucket beside my chair was essential. With all this one soon learned to recognise that John Brookes's overriding aim and ambition was to see his whole college brought together under one decent roof."*

The premises were a great test of leadership. 1944 marked 50 years since the School had moved into Church Street. The prospectus of 1944 has a map of the premises used by the Schools of Technology, Art and Commerce; in total they numbered 19.

How did JHB manage to communicate and meet with his colleagues across all these sites? In typically modest style, he travelled Oxford on a distinctive push bike, graduating to a moped. At least the Secretary of the Education Committee showed empathy, insisting that he should have a motor car and accordingly supplying a Wolseley. JHB reluctantly accepted it, thinking a bicycle was a more practical mode of transport in Oxford; he had difficulty in learning to drive and passing his test, and kept the same car for many years.

The governing body changed significantly during this period of feverish post-war activity. Wartime involvement in engineering had brought JHB and colleagues closer to the rapidly expanding Nuffield Organisation in Cowley. It was now a major industrial complex and JHB was at pains to develop a relationship with the company and its founder Lord Nuffield, whose connection stemmed from classes at the School many years previously.

George Dono joined the governors. He was a great ally for JHB and the first employer to sponsor part-time day release courses and later sandwich courses in engineering and science. A director of the Nuffield Organisation, he was Managing Director of Osberton Radiators, the Nuffield subsidiary based off the Woodstock Road, that was a key part of the automotive supply chain. Dono was the main protagonist in approaching the city Education Committee and the Ministry to enhance the buildings on the Cowley Road site for engineering and war-time production. He was also one of the main supporters in the final push for a new building. Other governors during this period included Dr George Kelly, Managing Director of the Pressed Steel Company, the other main manufacturing plant in Cowley, and representatives from smaller engineering companies, the building trades, architects, printing and the Trades Council. JHB sustained links with the University of Oxford and developed a relationship with a new major employer, the atomic research station at Harwell.

By the end of the war, it was generally agreed that the two and a half acres on the Cowley Road were inadequate. However the site continued to be developed, mainly for teaching engineering and building. This location was to be the home of the Oxford College of Further Education when it was created in 1961.

In the late 1940s many proposals were put forward for a new site. One was the proposed Nuffield College site in New Road, near to the town centre, if Lord Nuffield and the University of Oxford could be persuaded to build his newly endowed college on recently acquired land at Wytham. Another was the site of an old hospital on 11 acres of land opposite the Cowley Road site. However these were abandoned in favour of a 33-acre site on Headington Hill, which was part of the Morrell family estate, a seemingly virtuous circle as the family were benefactors in 1865. The Council purchased the site but as JHB later realised, *"The search had ended, but not the long delays and bitter disappointments over the actual building."*

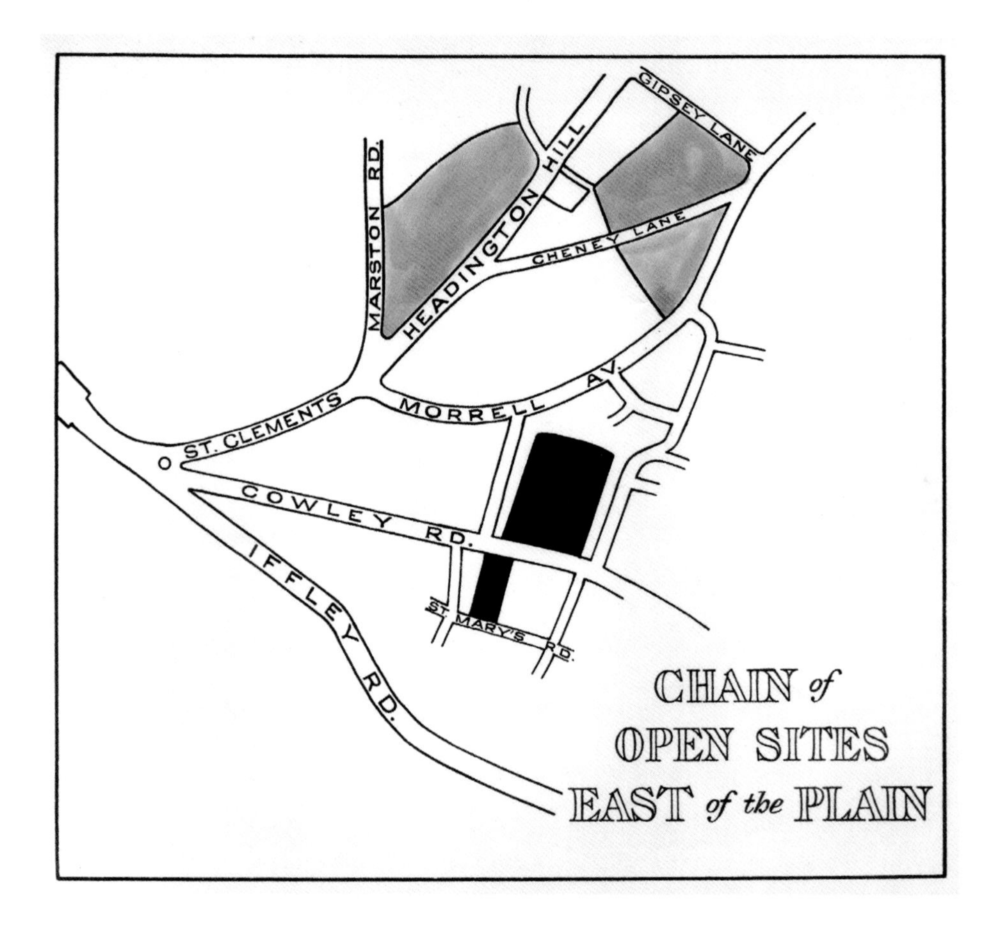

Possible locations of the proposed Headington site c1950.

Right: A press cutting from *Oxford Mail* in April 1949 showing JHB, second left and colleagues at an exhibition of the work of the School of Architecture.

Below left: The cover of a leaflet announcing the success of the School of Architecture and Building in being one of only 18 such courses to be exempt from the RIBA Final Examination in 1950.

OXFORD MAIL, FRIDAY, 29 APRIL, 1949

Oxford School of Architecture Exhibition at Black Hall, St.Giles's (L. to R.): COUN. K. WHEARE (chairman of governors), MR. J. H. BROOKES (Principal), MR. J. R. TOLSON (head of the School of Architecture) and MR. HAROLD S. ROGERS, who opened the exhibition yesterday, examining some of the exhibits.—(" O.M.")

SCHOOLS OF TECHNOLOGY ART AND COMMERCE, OXFORD

The School of Architecture and Building

FOUNDED 1929

Recognised by the R.I.B.A. as a Final School 1950

THE ROYAL INSTITUTE OF BRITISH ARCHITECTS informed the Governors of the Schools on the 23rd June, 1950, that it has approved the Visiting Board's recommendation that the School's five-year full-time course be recognised for the purpose of exemption from the R.I.B.A. Final Examination.

This recognition has been granted in the twenty-first year of the School's foundation, for it was in 1929 that the Education Committee sanctioned the appointment of a full-time studio instructor, Mr. S. N. Bertram, A.R.I.B.A. This followed a year of effort, chiefly on the part of Mr. R. Fielding Dodd, F.R.I.B.A., to encourage the number of young pupils and assistants in Oxford offices to support the new part-time courses which were established when the School of Art was re-organised in 1928. Until that

BECOMING A COLLEGE OF TECHNOLOGY

"Conditions for students are shockingly bad but the staff conditions were appalling", observed a Government Inspection in November 1947. In spite of the working conditions, the inspectors reported a very successful institution. They noted very good teamwork from the teaching staff, Heads of Department and Principal, and congratulated them: *"completely satisfactory; no bad teaching anywhere. Governors can be assured that they have a very good School."*

Chairman of the Governors, Kenneth Wheare, asked the inspectors about the interplay between technology, art and commerce, and was advised: *"This is to the advantage of students and staff that they can rub shoulders as often as possible."*

By 1950, student numbers had risen to over 4,000 and there were established departments of engineering, commerce, building, architecture, science and art. A department of catering had been established at Singletree House, Rose Hill in south-east Oxford.

JHB was proud of the School of Architecture and Building and he was particularly pleased when the Royal Institute of British Architects (RIBA) gave approval in June 1950 that the School's five-year, full-time course allowed students to be exempt from the Final RIBA examination. This was a great achievement in 21 years, given the beginnings were in such restricted circumstances. The Oxford course was one of only 18 nationally to be recognised in this way. In a celebratory paper, JHB paid tribute to the founding local architects, the excellence of the staff over the years and the debt owed to the Doric Club. So by this time, most of the educational subjects that form the basis of the current university had been established.

During this period, JHB and his colleagues spent many hours planning the layout of the Headington site. He had pursued a constant interest in college planning and design, regularly visiting and comparing other institutions such as Birmingham and Leicester. The 33 acres were to be used for both a college of technology and a secondary technical school. JHB's planning vision was based on his belief that the three areas of art, technology and commerce, should be complementary, and should have equal space and accommodation. This vision was translated into detailed plans that were approved by the City Education Committee in September 1949. The new college would serve the population of Oxford, then 220,000 people. The estimated capital expenditure on the scheme, planned to be built over five years, was £912,000 and the first phase was approved by the Ministry of Education.

A TERRIBLE BLOW

The City Council's Finance Committee developed a detailed financing proposal, which was put before a meeting of the full City Council. To the supporters' utter astonishment, the proposal was rejected by 38 votes to 20. The arguments rested on four main points: affordability and the potential increase on the rates; the diversion of funds from house building; the money needed for defence; and the fact that Oxford was not an industrial area. This last point must have particularly infuriated the Nuffield Organisation as well as JHB. Generally, the population of Oxford was outraged by the decision. Letters and articles flowed into the local press commenting *"I can't think that this is going to be ruinous to Oxford"* and *"not a single house will be lost"*.

Press cuttings from *Oxford Mail* of September 1950 expressing public protest at the Oxford City Council's decision.

Below right: A ball point sketch drawing, perhaps by JHB, of the initial plan for the new buildings in Headington c1950. It is remarkably similar to what would be built.

OXFORD MAIL, TUESDAY,

)xford call for public protest City Council

TECHNICAL COLLEGE VOTE STRONGLY CRITICISED

A CALL to all those interested in further education in Oxford to register a protest against Oxford City Council's rejection of the Education Committee's proposal to build the first block of a College of Further Education was made by Coun. K. C. Wheare at the Education Committee meeting yesterday.

OXFORD'S LOST OPPORTUNITY

OXFORD City Council yesterday took a very grave and, in our view, a very unwise decision in rejecting the Education Committee's proposal to build the first block of a College for Further Education at an estimated cost of £250,000. Critics of the scheme based their opposition on two main grounds—that housing was a more urgent priority and that the City cannot afford the cost. We do not doubt the sincerity of those who urged the rejection of the proposal but we find their arguments unconvincing. Take the first one. No-one who knows anything about the appalling suffering and discomfort due to the shortage of accommodation in Oxford would wish to hold up the housing programme, but the fact of the matter is that the rejection of the College scheme will not mean the erection of a single additional house in Oxford. For the Ministry promise of a grant was for a specific purpose, and if that is rejected then the money will be diverted to the cause of further education elsewhere. It will not be spent on housing in Oxford.

We have consistently urged rigorous economy in municipal and national expenditure, and the cutting out of all unnecessary expenditure. But unlike the money recently cheerfully voted for floodlighting the City and for paying for a Festival of Britain organiser, this proposed expenditure was not unnecessary. In the first place the Council is bound to provide for further education. If this rejection of the proposal is final it will mean that many people in this area desiring further education will have to go to Reading. Oxford will have to pay the fees—and their travelling expenses. And this is Oxford, the seat of learning! Recognition of the importance of technical education has been tardy, but it is now admitted. And anyone who takes the slightest interest in the subject knows that the scattered, inadequate premises which have been the home of further education in Oxford for so many years are a standing disgrace to the City. As for the demand for such instruction it was an eye-opener to see the enormous queues of would-be students waiting to enrol for evening classes which thronged the Town Hall and its precincts last night. The ironical thing about yesterday's vote is that it is only a year since the Council approved the Further Education Committee's scheme. Now it has completely reversed its policy and lost an opportunity which may never recur. We regard yesterday's vote as unfortunate and shortsighted.

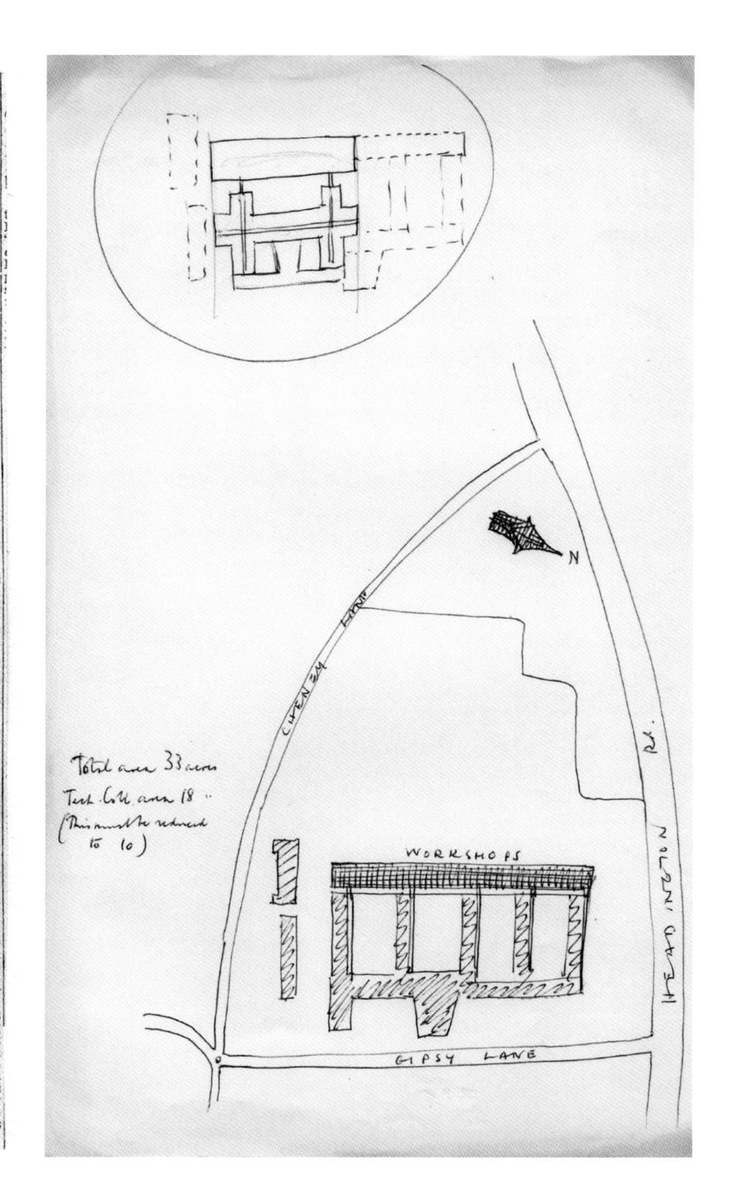

Councillor Lodge, a prominent Oxford businessman and chairman of the Education Committee, reminded councillors that the Investment Committee of the Treasury had budgeted for money specifically dedicated to technical education:

> *"Other local authorities are clamouring throughout the country for allocations for technical schemes. If Oxford's opportunity is rejected, no further opportunity may occur: we have a priority for a scheme which is not only a local necessity but is in the national interest."*

The Oxford Times captured the spirit in the leader of 22 September 1950, entitled Waste Paper:

> *"most local authorities make some curious decisions in their time, but we cannot recall one so astonishing as the City Council's flat rejection on Monday of the proposed College of Further Education. For nearly forty years the importance of such a college to replace the scattered and obsolete buildings of the Schools of Technology, Art and Commerce has been generally accepted... It seems almost incredible that such a thing could happen in Oxford, which should be in the forefront in educational matters... the VOLTE-FACE is fantastic."*

After examining the local impact of the Council's rejection, the leader writer finished by setting the decision in a national context:

> *"The demand for young men and women with advanced technical training has never been so great as it is now, when our national survival depends on industry being able to compete on the best of terms with the highly scientific methods in world markets. But Oxford, says the Council now, shall not train them - and despite the fact that the Council had itself planned the provision of the College."*

JHB's governors and close supporters now came to the fore to challenge what they considered to be a disastrous mistake by the City Council.

Below left: A cartoon from the Oxford press by Alan Course, in September 1950.

Below right: A press cutting from *Oxford Mail* of September 1950 announcing plans for a Citizens' Meeting at the Town Hall.

"Well, we can always use the ground for a cycle-speedway or a pitch-and-toss school, or something!"

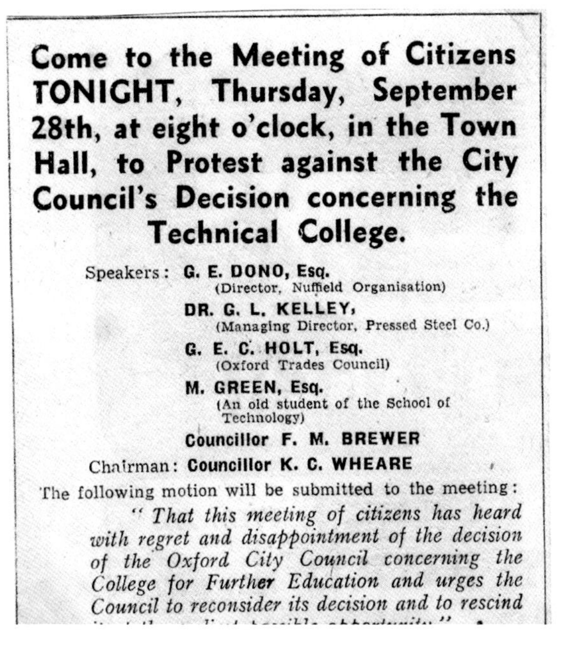

Come to the Meeting of Citizens TONIGHT, Thursday, September 28th, at eight o'clock, in the Town Hall, to Protest against the City Council's Decision concerning the Technical College.

Speakers: **G. E. DONO, Esq.** (Director, Nuffield Organisation)
DR. G. L. KELLEY, (Managing Director, Pressed Steel Co.)
G. E. C. HOLT, Esq. (Oxford Trades Council)
M. GREEN, Esq. (An old student of the School of Technology)
Councillor F. M. BREWER

Chairman: **Councillor K. C. WHEARE**

The following motion will be submitted to the meeting:

"That this meeting of citizens has heard with regret and disappointment of the decision of the Oxford City Council concerning the College for Further Education and urges the Council to reconsider its decision and to rescind

Kenneth Wheare, the longtime supporter of JHB, issued a call to protest against the Council's rejection. Writing about this occasion he recalled:

> *"I had been assured of so much support for the proposal in circles outside the City Council that I felt the City Council must be wrong; that it had misjudged public opinion. So to my own surprise, I found myself proclaiming that a protest of the citizens would be organised against the City Council's decision. We called a meeting in the Town Hall and we had so many supporters that the Council Chamber was filled, the main committee room was also filled and there was an overflow meeting on the staircase."*

The meeting was held on the 28 September 1950, convened by Councillor Wheare, with a main speech by George Dono, who had a special message of support from Lord Nuffield. Other speakers include Dr George Kelly of Pressed Steel, Mr G E Holt of the Oxford Trades Council, and Councillor Frederick Brewer. The meeting, with much popular support, adopted a resolution calling on the City Council to rescind its decision not to build a new college. JHB's other close supporter, Charles Batey, now Printer to the University and a Governor, wrote a letter to the *Oxford Mail* published on 13 October 1950:

> *"I returned from America late on Wednesday, a week ago and awoke on Thursday morning to find the City quivering with excitement of a controversy such as it has not known through all the 22 years of my residence here."*

The City Council were vexed and challenged. Views were not on established party lines, nor did they reflect any town-gown divide. Some councillors, in the aftermath of World War Two and with the advent of the Korean War (1950-1953), were deeply concerned about reserving funds for defence, reflecting national as well as local concern.

At the Annual Speech Day on 9 November 1950, JHB reflected on the City Council's decision before a large gathering in Rhodes House. He was no doubt deeply disappointed but continued his campaign, quoting a colleague: *"We will teach our students on the steps of the Martyrs' Memorial if need be."*

He concluded his Principal's Report with words that illustrate his undaunted and statesman-like character:

> *"We have fought this battle repeatedly; we will now have to fight it again, and we shall not have lost it until the spirit of despondency has weakened our resolve. We have improvised successfully for several generations and we shall go on improvising until we have convinced our fellow citizens that a College of Further Education is a proud possession rather than a burdensome and unnecessary luxury. That day may not come in my time, but it will assuredly come during the working lifetime of most of you."*

With such outstanding support and deep sense of purpose, it was only a matter of time. In late October 1951 the Education Committee again put the scheme to the full Council. Unfortunately the matter was deferred for a further twelve months during which time various modifications were made to the scheme. During this short period, policy had changed with a more positive attitude towards educational spending, and funds for education from central government were more freely available. On 28 July 1952, the revised plans were approved without discussion by the City Council.

In fact, the School would become the Oxford College of Technology, Art and Commerce in its new Headington home, while the Cowley Road site would be home to the College of Further Education when it was created in 1961.

The first major building investment on the Headington site since the 1950s faced similar planning tussles but In 2010, approval was given for a new library and teaching building for Oxford Brookes University. The new building is now aptly named the John Henry Brookes Building.

THE PROMISED LAND

Monday 5 April 1954 was a momentous day for JHB with the laying of the foundation stone of the new College of Technology, Art and Commerce. The ceremony was appropriately performed by Lord Nuffield, founder of the Nuffield Organisation, alumnus and long-time supporter of the College.

In his address, JHB warmly thanked the founding and current governors, benefactors, the University of Oxford and its distinguished supporters, Oxford City Council, the Education Committee and colleagues past and present. He reminded the gathering of the positive

OXFORD MAIL, TUESDAY, APRIL 6, 1954

New Oxford college stone laying

The Sheriff of Oxford (Coun. R. E. Warrell), Lord and Lady Nuffield and the Mayor of Oxford (Coun. A. B. Brown) at the College of Technology, Art and Commerce foundation-stone laying.

Left: A press cutting from *Oxford Mail* in April 1954 announcing the stone laying of the new college by Lord Nuffield (1877-1963).

contribution that past students had made to the economy, no doubt referring in part to the guest of honour. He concluded with a very poignant sentiment:

> *"...Church Street, St Ebbe's was a place of happy and blessed memory... We may agree with all who hold that magnificent work is often done in poor and out of date buildings; but that will not prevent us from taking our place when the time comes in a splendid, well equipped and up to date building where we can show that even better work can be done of lasting benefit to the City, the neighbourhood and the country as a whole."*

In 1954 the Junior Technical School moved from St Ebbe's to become Cheney School, a secondary technical school sited next to the new College. By September 1955 the technical areas of the College - engineering, architecture and building - had moved into new workshops and classrooms. This was celebrated by a series of open days for the public to inspect the buildings and an official visit was made by the Lord Mayor, Aldermen and Councillors on 16 September 1955.

The building work continued over the next few years and gradually departments moved from Church Street and elsewhere into their new quarters.

But by now, JHB had reached retirement age and although he was granted an extra year at the helm by the Education Committee, he duly retired in 1956.

FAREWELL
DINNER TO

John H. Brookes

given by the Governors
and members of Staff of the
College of Technology Art
and Commerce, Oxford
at the Assembly Room
Town Hall, Oxford

5 JULY 1956

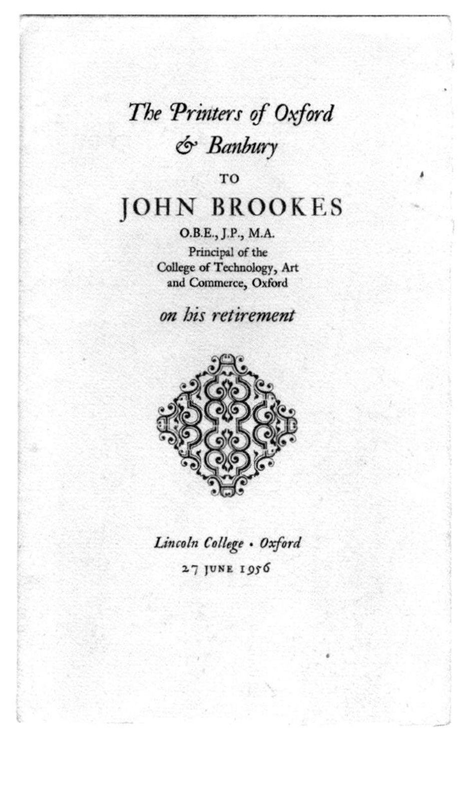

The Printers of Oxford
& Banbury
TO
JOHN BROOKES
O.B.E., J.P., M.A.
Principal of the
College of Technology, Art
and Commerce, Oxford
on his retirement

Lincoln College · Oxford
27 JUNE 1956

Two invitations from the 17 retirement parties organised for JHB in 1956.

AN INSPIRING CHARACTER
1956 – 1975

Previous page:
A portrait of JHB taken in the 1950s.

Opposite: A photograph of JHB and his friend, sometime colleague and neighbour Basil Kohler, at the tennis courts at Bury Knowle Park, Headington in the 1930s.

AN INSPIRING CHARACTER 1956 – 1975

There is no doubt that JHB was respected, admired and loved. The welter of letters and press articles generated at the time of his retirement were capped by seventeen retirement parties. These were thrown by departments of the College, industry associations, community groups, and the local authority with an official farewell at the Oxford Town Hall. JHB noted in a letter that he must be the best fed man in Oxford.

JHB's involvement in the Oxford community had begun soon after he came to the city in 1928. A number of his activities were directly related to the School and his professional interests - national art and teaching associations, reaching out to industry through business clubs, and using his skills and experience to help young people. He was involved with the City Council Youth Committee, the YMCA, encouraging and training youth leaders and young people to take up some form of education, such as evening classes.

JHB met many people, engaging extensively through professional associations and clubs. He was a consummate networker and knew the value of encouraging visitors to his classrooms and the advantages of newspaper reports of successes. He established many contacts for the benefit of the School and his students. But he also formed deep and abiding friendships; many of his own early mentors became lifelong friends, as did many of his colleagues. He believed that social life was an important parallel to work, and together they enriched careers and lives. He had experienced the success of this and developed his enthusiasm for a more communal way of life at the Guild of Handicraft. He included his students in social activities and encouraged trying new things, through classes, sports and physical activity, reading, public speaking and acting.

JHB was a caring, thoughtful father but his career and extra-curricular activities were clearly demanding of his time. JHB and Helena seemed to have managed their family life in a successful manner and, practising the ways of the Guild, JHB seems to have seamlessly integrated his working life with his social life. Colleagues and students would travel with him and his family on holidays, both local camping trips and more adventurous travel and cruises abroad. Joan recalls holidays on a farm in Standlake run by the Clack family; her father, brother, staff and students would all be there, camping under canvas. JHB did not routinely make time for sport but loved walking and being outdoors. He was also a keen gardener and his garden at the Gate House was the pride of the neighbourhood.

Both his children developed successful careers. Joan decided to follow the family tradition and trained as a nursery teacher. She remained at home throughout World War Two and eventually moved to Birmingham to take up a headship. She never married and led a quiet life at home surrounded by her father's artwork. After school, Peter started a course at the School of Architecture but when war broke out in 1939, he volunteered for the Royal Air Force, in marked contrast to his father a generation earlier. Peter had a 'successful war' as a fighter pilot. He married a German woman and lived in Germany for the rest of his life. JHB and Helena kept in close contact with both Joan and Peter after they left home. They spent several holidays in Germany, JHB making many drawings and paintings of the countryside. Peter and his wife Gertrude and son Joachim often visited Oxford.

JHB used his full range of skills to support his community activities. Throughout his life he was a member, director, chairman, founder or president of at least forty organisations, including professional art and educational bodies, many youth organisations and the City of

Above: A photograph of a group of staff and students from the School's catering department based at Singletree House, Rose Hill at a formal occasion in the 1950s. JHB in white tie, is standing on the far right.

Right: A celebratory dinner menu of the Rotary Club of Oxford for 26 February 1945 designed by JHB.

THE ROTARY CLUB OF OXFORD

DINNER

to celebrate the

21st Anniversary of the Club

(Charter granted 26th February, 1924)

THE RANDOLPH HOTEL, OXFORD

MONDAY, 26th FEBRUARY, 1945

6.45 for 7 p.m.

Oxford Education Committee. He was also a magistrate, becoming Chairman of the Bench, a visitor and teacher at Oxford Prison, a visitor at the local Campsfield Detention Centre, active member of a number of music and drama associations, and a founder of the Oxford Management Club and a lifelong Rotarian.

He'd learned to rise at 5.30am each day as a farm worker in World War One when he was registered as a conscientious objector. As Principal, his schedule was always taxing, and without continuing this habit of an early start, he would probably not have been able to complete his duties. His dedication to good causes was unquenchable, particularly in support of young people. Perhaps a sense of guilt pervaded JHB's thoughts and actions, a sense born from his conscientious objector status of World War One.

The Oxford Rotary Club was one of his deepest involvements. It fulfilled a charitable purpose but also brought JHB into regular contact with leading local figures from the university and Oxford businesses. JHB was President in 1939/40 and Chairman in 1945/46. His resignation letter, after he had received health warnings in the spring of 1975, was heartfelt. He was awarded its highest honour, Honorary Membership, for his *"unstinting time, devotion and hard work and encouragement to others who tried to follow his footsteps."* JHB's involvement in these bodies was not one of passive membership but of commitment, using all his gifts to help fulfil the organisation's aims. He usually became a leading light, skilfully chairing meetings, giving speeches, and often writing and designing communications and identities.

After World War Two, JHB served as a Justice of the Peace from 1946 to 1963. He started on the Juvenile Panel, moving to join the senior Bench, and eventually succeeding Sir Basil Blackwell in 1961 as Chief Magistrate. Blackwell, son of the bookshop's founder, was a great supporter of JHB and they had known each other probably since the early 1920s. They became firm friends and colleagues on the Bench. Sir Basil expressed a wise summary of JHB's character:

> *"Here was one at peace with himself, with eyes for beauty and hands exactly trained to reproduce it. His was the serenity of the craftsman, self disciplined to 'get it right'; so he could give his whole mind to the matter in hand. This serenity as it seemed to me was informed by the Stoic rule: 'Love your fellow man and do him good'. I would come away from such conferences with a sense of purification."*

In another story from this time, a demobbed major arrived at the Church Street, St Ebbe's building for an interview. Seeing a small and seemingly unimportant man at the door, he haughtily handed over his belongings, perhaps a portfolio, requesting that he carry them up to the Principal's office. He followed the small man up the stairs and was shown into the room. The small man was of course JHB, who proceeded to interview him, no doubt fairly and with good humour.

Another good friend, Charles Broadhurst, President of the Oxford stationers Hunt and Broadhurst, and a fellow artist, recorded:

> *"As a magistrate he [JHB] put in a considerable amount of time at Oxford's prison where he ran a modest but flourishing art class among the prisoners. Apparently there was one prisoner whose keenness and certain aptitude he had thought to encourage by giving him some of my drawings to copy. Being John, it worried him that he had not sought my approval before parting with these drawings; even more was the guilty thought that he would probably never have told me this; but then (with his special brand of humour coming through) he told me that he had now to confess, because the prisoner with the*

JHB, his wife Helena (right) and daughter Joan (left) photographed in formal attire on his visit to Buckingham Palace to receive an OBE. The photograph was used by the Oxford press in February 1953.

budding artistic talent had escaped during the night, and had taken my drawings with him."

JHB shared his public spiritedness with his father, who was deeply motivated by his Christianity, but JHB wasn't particularly religious. He would have described himself as an agnostic. His political views were liberal; Joan records that he supported the Labour Party, although not overtly, and generally voted that way. He was deeply caring and public-spirited, and his dedication to his fellow man was extraordinary.

JHB's determination and achievements in his professional life and commitment to the community and young people were rewarded with an OBE in the New Year Honours List of January 1953.

The year of his retirement, 1956, saw the establishment he had so comprehensively led become the Oxford College of Technology. The official opening of the College in Headington was some time later on 15 November 1963 with the Duke of Edinburgh as the guest of honour. JHB was no doubt disappointed not to be leading the College when the vision he had set was eventually realised. His had been a journey of almost thirty years of tireless effort to establish applied education on a firm base, housed in appropriate new buildings. In his speech at the official opening, he described his time as "lean years", ending his speech:

"To those of us who had survived the hardships of the lean years, it seemed scarcely believable that we were now allowed to set foot inside the promised land. Gone were the fears and hesitancies of the past, to be replaced by a city's pride in a new College of Technology."

During his retirement, he enjoyed returning to teaching and lecturing at schools and the College, chairing and participating in professional societies, increasing his community involvement, expressing his views regularly in both the local and national press, writing reflective books and returning to his great joy of drawing and painting.

Writing in 1970, in the staff magazine, he noted prophetically:

"I have been privileged to see from the outside, fourteen years of achievement which no doubt others will someday record. But that will only take us to the birth of the Oxford Polytechnic."

He had overseen the development of an institution that would go on to greater things and took a modest satisfaction in knowing that his years of effort had been worthwhile. John Henry Brookes died following a short illness on 29 September 1975.

APPRECIATION OF HIS LIFE

The significance of life was well understood, both during his lifetime and for a period after his death. In 1970, the College had become Oxford Polytechnic. The staff and students of the Departments of Publishing and Design published *John Henry Brookes Craftsman Educator Administrator,* in 1979, edited by A Stuart Addison, which included tributes from Sir Kenneth Wheare and Sir Basil Blackwell.

In 1980, an institutional history, *Genesis to Maturity 1865–1980*, was written by alumna Elaine Henry. She reflected, *"Any history of the institutions which preceded Oxford Polytechnic begins, after the 1920s, to take on something of the nature of a paean of praise for John Brookes."*

During his lifetime JHB was a consistently popular figure. The family papers contain a file, with his handwritten title, 'Appreciations'. It consists of references, some for job applications, others on the occasion of his retirement, and letters from friends and influential people singing his praises. Another file holds the letters received by Helena, Joan and Peter after JHB died. They show the respect and affection in which he was held:

"The most charming and selfless man I knew"

"One who perceives mankind with a kindly and judicious spirit"

"A devoted and sagacious advisor"

"Steadfast, patient and valiant"

"We are all the better for having known him"

"A man without false pride and most unassuming in manner, who could nonetheless be as firm as a rock when the occasion demanded"

"A man who got his priorities in life absolutely right"

"My own life was made richer by his existence"

"I mourn him as the best, the kindest and the truest friend I ever had"

So this is a story of a remarkable man whose educational leadership in Oxford influenced the lives of thousands of young people. Countless designers, architects, engineers, surveyors, accountants, administrators, craftsmen of many kinds and business people developed their vocations and careers, having benefited from JHB's outlook.

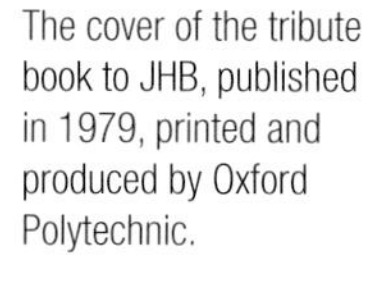

The cover of the tribute book to JHB, published in 1979, printed and produced by Oxford Polytechnic.

PART TWO
REFLECTIONS ON THE 40TH ANNIVERSARY OF HIS DEATH

THE ARTIST AND CRAFTSMAN

Previous page: JHB photographed c1915 when an art and design student in Leicester.

Below left: A bookplate designed by JHB for his father Robert Brookes (1866-1938), probably c1915 when he was an art and design student. His father was well known for playing the flute.

Below right: One of the first Christmas cards by JHB in 1917. He continued to design greetings cards for his family and friends throughout his life.

THE ARTIST AND CRAFTSMAN

As a young man, the challenge of earning a living with a young family and the draw of his educational ideals, meant that JHB was not to pursue an artistic career. One of the questions that I have often been asked since I started my research into JHB's life is how good an artist would JHB have been?

THE ARTISTIC ENDEAVOUR

JHB was a very competent artist and craftsman with a well-developed visual sense. He had two main periods of artistic endeavour. The first ran from 1909 until 1924 while he was at Leicester School of Art and the Guild of Handicraft. A second period followed his retirement in 1956 and continued until his death.

The influence of the Arts and Crafts Movement was profound on JHB, shaping his ideals and his educational policies. But his thorough training in the skills of drawing and lettering, as well as sculpture and silversmithing, were also shaped by the arts and crafts approach. Since his death, his artistic output is as much part of his reputation as his years as Principal.

From an early age, JHB showed a keen interest in art and architecture. He had a broadly based artistic training at the Leicester School of Art, and today we would call him multi-disciplined. His exam drawings of 1914 show a highly proficient, academic ability; they are very good examples of a particular style of life drawing. At art school he also developed his lifelong interest in lettering and letter forms, initially as drawn lettering and later as carved form.

A detail of JHB's stone carved relief of angels on the portico of St Alban's Church in Charles Street, Oxford made in 1933.

At the Guild of Handicraft summer schools, he learnt a range of craft skills, particularly silversmithing under the tutelage of George Hart. He produced some fine pieces in the arts and crafts style, several hallmarked in Birmingham in 1914. After World War One, working as an assistant to Alec Miller, he became a very competent carver in wood and stone. Most of Miller's work was commissioned from ecclesiastical clients working on churches and on war memorials and it seems that JHB specialised in letter cutting.

His middle years, filled with his teaching and administrative duties, didn't leave much time for his own work. He was commissioned to carve the entrance portico, a beautiful low relief of angels, to St Alban's Church in Charles Street, Oxford, which was dedicated in May 1933. The interior Stations of the Cross carvings were made by the well-known but controversial sculptor Eric Gill, who JHB probably met in Chipping Campden. He developed a sound knowledge of architecture, which he shared with many colleagues and friends, and he became an accomplished architectural historian and critic.

JHB continued to make drawings and occasional paintings and prints of architectural and landscape subjects. He also regularly designed greetings and Christmas cards, from his student days until the end of his life. In 1952 he had a water colour of St Giles' Church, Horspath, a village just outside Oxford, accepted for the Royal Academy Summer Exhibition. It seems that he didn't continue silversmith work and did very little carving in his later years, although he occasionally repaired lettering.

A silver stone-encrusted fruit bowl made by JHB in the arts and crafts style in 1914.

A watercolour of St Giles' Church, Horspath by JHB. It was accepted by the Royal Academy for its Summer Exhibition in 1952.

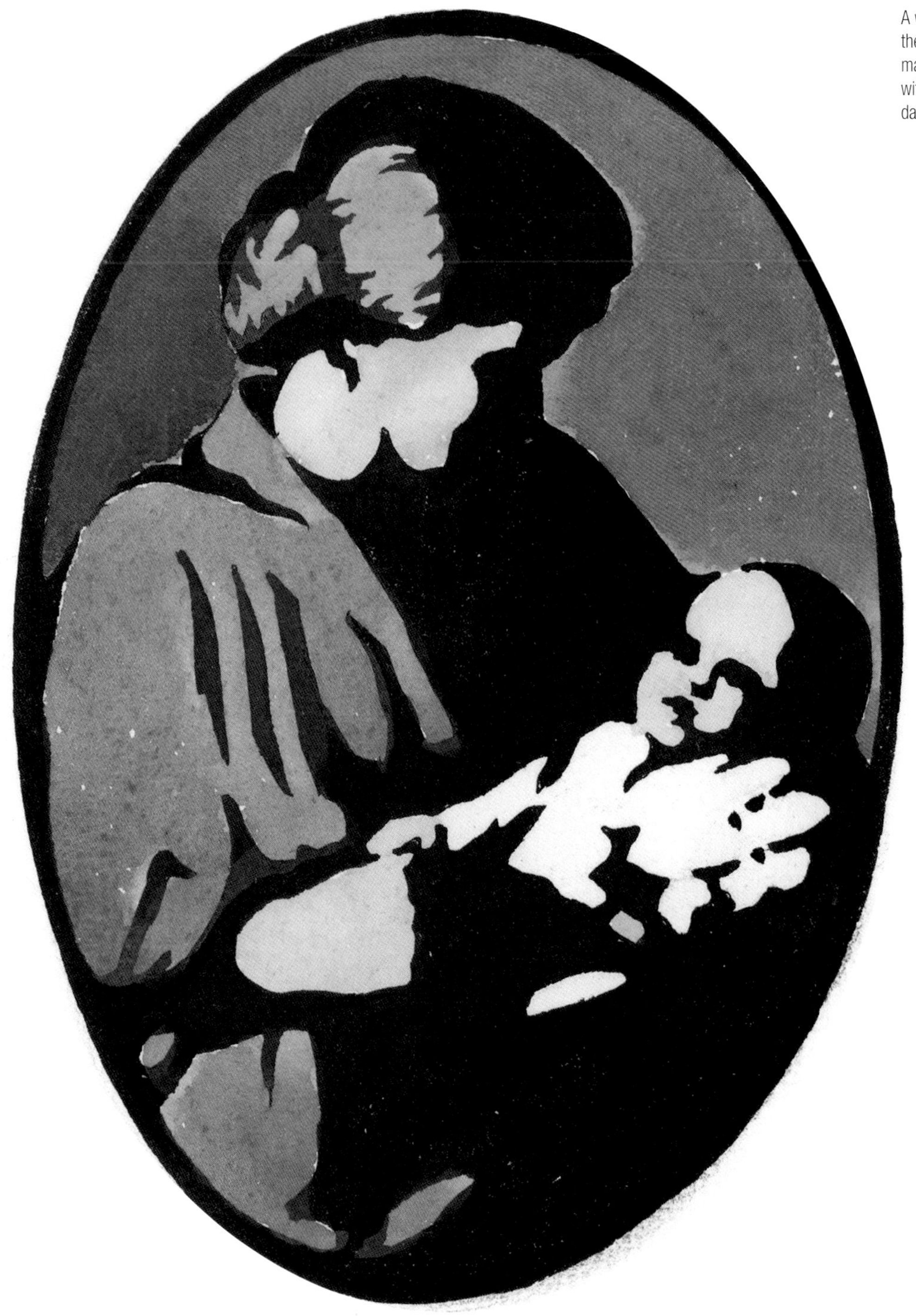

A watercolour design in the form of a cartouche made by JHB of his wife Helena and daughter Joan in 1920.

Whenever an opportunity arose to design material for one of the organisations with which he was involved, JHB took it on. He designed several annual report covers for the School, and subsequently the College, as well as identities for many organisations including Oxford City Council. JHB aimed for a high standard of visual communication; where he did not design himself, he maintained a guiding hand. He was in effect an early design manager, overseeing style and consistency and the quality of the printing.

In the years after his retirement in 1956, JHB's output was prodigious. He was always drawing and painting. He had a studio in his garden at the Gate House but he worked mostly on the kitchen table. His interest seemed to be in the craft of producing the image, for when it was finished he lost interest. He gave away much of his work and there are many stories of admiring onlookers being made a gift of a drawing or painting when he was working outside.

In 1957, *The Oxford Times* commissioned him to produce drawings for its leader page. They were of village, town and city streets, churches, country views and distinctive buildings around Oxford. He continued to produce them weekly for 15 years, with his 100th drawing, of Holywell Street, Oxford, published on 2 August 1968. His work was always precise and disciplined with great attention to detail, published with a caption usually describing the history of the scene and often with a perceptive comment on the architecture. In particular JHB loved the Cotswold vernacular and the pre-eminence of Oxford's buildings; he was always looking for new perspectives and new views. In retirement one of his favourite occupations was to take his car and spend a day sketching.

JHB wrote and illustrated five books. The first three books were published and printed as student exercises in the Printing Department. The books are carefully researched, with informative commentary on the countryside and villages near Oxford. They are partly autobiographical, relating to his fondly-remembered years in the Cotswolds, local holidays and commentary on buildings that he liked and some that he did not. They include his reflection on a visit to Blenheim Palace with his friend Thomas Rayson, who was responsible for repairs to the palace:

> *"I started on a sketch of a subject with which I was to some extent out of sympathy. But before long mass and weight became a little more coherent, and for the first time I felt the truth of John Summerson's observation on Blenheim Palace: 'something of the Gothic fortress is wrought into a sombre and magnificent classic unity'. Nevertheless it still seemed most oppressive; a formal and lifeless exercise in composition and balance on a colossal and terrifying scale."*

Sir John Vanburgh's English Baroque-style edifice divides architectural opinion today as it did in the 1720s when it was built, with JHB clearly on the side of the dissenters, disliking its grandeur and ostentation.

The last two books were published commercially by a friend, Bernard Crossland. The second of these, *North Oxfordshire Churches*, was published in the year of JHB's death, 1975, another example of his ceaseless energy.

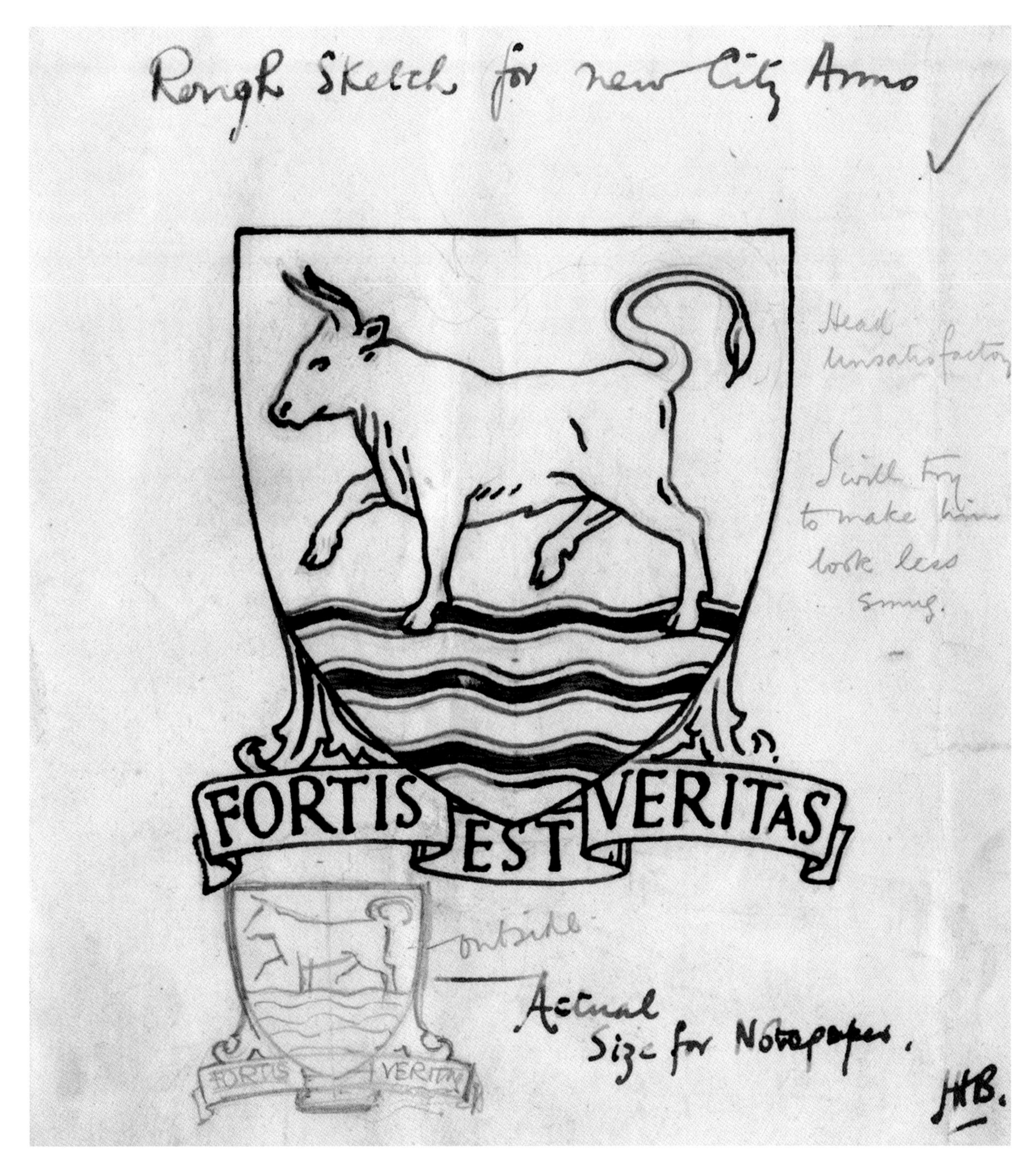

JHB's design sketches for the Oxford City Arms made shortly after his arrival in Oxford in 1929. His note reads "I will try to make him look less smug".

Right: The prospectus cover of 1929/30 with the bull looking less smug.

Far right: A JHB design in scraper-board for The Arts Guild; one of the many organisations of which he was a member, probably made in the 1950s.

Below: The covers of JHB's five books, written, published and printed in his retirement years.

ARTISTIC ACCOMPLISHMENT

So did JHB's professional choice to become a teacher and educational leader mean that we lost an artist of great potential? My view is that he was a very competent, figurative artist and a highly accomplished craftsman but he was not outstanding. His early work at art school and at the Guild of Handicraft was of a high standard, but perhaps inevitably his later work, although skilful, was as a hobbyist.

The second decade of the 20th century, when JHB was at the Leicester School of Art and the Guild, was the most explosive that the art world has ever experienced. It produced major artistic figures such as Picasso, Matisse, Braque and many others. It witnessed Cubism, Fauvism and Surrealism, Marcel Duchamp and Dada, abstraction and the birth of modern art.

However JHB's work and visual style were a product of his art school training and the pervading influence of the Arts and Crafts Movement. Some of his close friends of the same generation, like Basil Kohler, a neighbour, fellow artist and teaching colleague, endorsed modernism and embraced it in their work. Others, like Alec Miller and Tom Rayson, did not and were fervent believers in traditional ways.

JHB made sure his students were able to explore modern art through visiting lecturers, practitioners and borrowed pieces, but he did not embrace it in his own work. To some extent, this may have been an inevitable result of his art education. British art school training in the early 20th century was as it had been for many hundreds of years, a somewhat formulaic teaching of drawing and painting. Most art examinations were based on attaining set techniques of drawing.

JHB photographed at home for *Oxford Mail* on the occasion of his 80th birthday. He is looking reflectively at sculpture and silverware made during his time at the Guild of Handicraft.

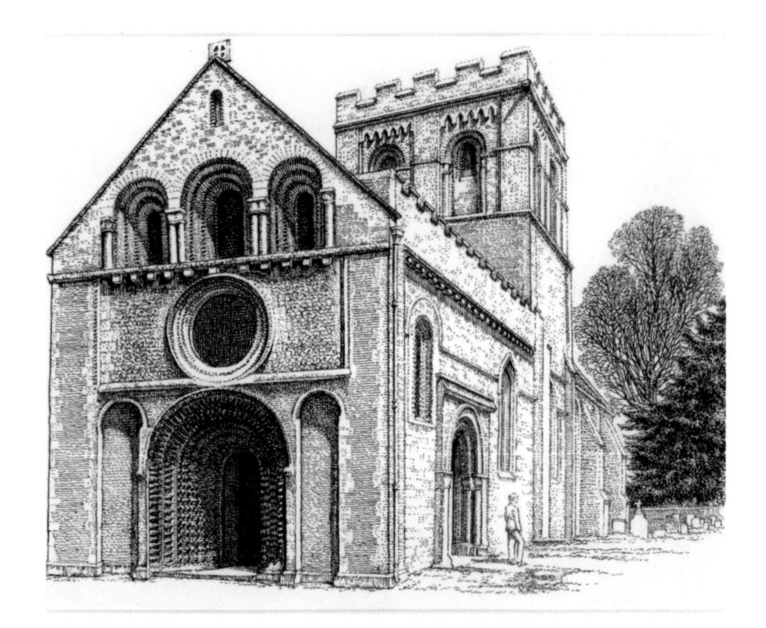

Top left: A pen and ink drawing of the west front of the fine example of a Norman church, St Mary's, Iffley, Oxford probably drawn in the 1950s.

Top right: A pen and ink drawing of a memorial.

Right: A pen and ink drawing of a gate and pastoral scene reminiscent of the style of his drawing mentor, Fred Griggs.

Opposite; A well composed scraper-board of the harbour at Rozel, Jersey made by JHB when on holiday. Scraper-board is a technique using sharp tools to etch into a board coated with a thin layer of white China clay coated with black India ink. It originated in the 19th century in Britain and France and was popular from the 1930s to the 1950s, particularly for illustration.

When interviewed on the occasion of his 80th birthday in 1971, JHB was remarkably critical:

> *"Art students are much better trained today than we were. When I think back to my own training I can only describe it as pernicious. It was training in manipulative ability and nothing else. I don't ever remember anyone pointing out to me that painting was a matter of inspiration and imagination. Perhaps my life might have taken a different course if they had."*

I think that JHB's memory was somewhat unfair to his teachers, most of whom he greatly respected. His comments on the pernicious, manipulative training were probably focused on the syllabus and the need to teach drawing in a set manner for examination purposes, which was soon to change. However JHB mastered these techniques and partly funded his education by teaching drawing himself. He won several scholarships and passed several exams in craft subjects at Leicester, a pioneering college in applied art and design.

In all aspects of his life, JHB showed sound judgement. Of his own abilities, based on his extensive knowledge of art, he concluded in the same reflective interview:

> *"I have no illusions about my drawings. They are not art or anything like that. They are reports of things for which I have a real love or affection."*

He also ponders his career:

> *"I have no regrets but I often wish that instead of being a 'Jack of all trades' I had been a master of one. A writer, a painter, a sculptor, a silversmith – it really wouldn't have mattered what."*

Although a good judge of his own abilities, he was also innately modest. He was competent at all those crafts. But he was a 'master' of educational leadership. In that, JHB undoubtedly found his vocation.

REVIVING HIS LEGACY

Previous page: A portrait of JHB, probably taken in the 1950s.

REVIVING HIS LEGACY

That the culture of Oxford Brookes today often unknowingly still derives from JHB's warmth, determination and ideals with such longevity, is in itself a testament to him. But somehow in the years since his death in 1975, while his name lives on in the title of Oxford Brookes University, his profound impact on the city and its people has become a lost tale. So I wanted to capture JHB's personal values and explore how his life's work has great relevance and can provide guidance in the 21st century.

PERSONAL VALUES AND INFLUENCE

JHB's story reflects the continuing lack of commitment to applied education in Britain which in my opinion, continues. JHB understood the vital importance of technology to a successful economy. British politicians and administrators did not in the past and do not today champion or sufficiently invest in applied, vocational or technological education to help build and sustain our economy. The prevailing culture continues to focus on academic prowess rather than championing skills which more readily lead to innovation and entrepreneurship.

JHB's achievement is all the more remarkable as art-trained leaders in tertiary education are rare beings. You can count such people on the fingers of one hand. Perhaps if there had been more people of JHB's calibre, public opinion would have changed and technical education, the UK workforce and the British economy would be in a stronger position.

To sustain his vision over such an extended period took firm educational ideas drawn from his own life and education experiences. But what were JHB's personal strengths and values?

First, I put practicality and craftsmanship. He was determined that things, processes as well as artefacts, should be made to the highest standards of human endeavour. His influences were his family forebears and his father; it was in his genes. This was then honed and developed by his art and craft education and the Guild of Handicraft.

Second, are self-improvement and ambition, a powerful Victorian characteristic, aimed at his own life in a modest way, but particularly for his students. He believed in the capacity of humans to do good things, whatever their starting point in life.

Third, fellowship and generosity. JHB had a great sensitivity for his fellow beings, making him a good teacher. He formed strong relationships and had an innate sense of fairness and respect for others. He understood that sometimes the only way to overcome challenges is to face them with humour. Many of those I spoke to during my research recall a twinkle in his eye. He was forever generous with his time and support given to so many organisations and friends.

I wonder how would JHB have reacted to 21st-century life? Although a craftsman in all he did, I think he would have embraced new technology as he embraced innovation and change in his own time. I think he would be very concerned for the under-privileged in such an affluent society and saddened by youth unemployment. His thoughts on wealth creation and a highly skilled working population are still relevant, perhaps more so in high-tech modern Oxford than in many other cities.

To really understand how much his story is part of Oxford's modern history, many fortunate individuals who came under his educational spell have recounted their memories of JHB to me.

I first met JHB in 1964 in my Lower Sixth year at Cheney School. I recall a small, seemingly reserved man being introduced by my art master, Kenneth Wade. He had a small portfolio under his arm and had come to the school to deliver a talk to the sixth form art group. He proceeded to talk, I was to learn, about one of his favourite subjects, lettering. From his portfolio he produced a number of drawn examples of his own work. One in particular I recall was taken from the Trajan Column in Rome, which is considered the definitive Roman lettering. I remember him enthusiastically talking about the proportions, the form of the serifs, the thicks and thins and the critically important letter spacing. He was inspirational and the whole class was enthralled.

JHB was an influence on my own life, but it was not until 1992, the time Oxford gained its second university, and over the past few years researching his life, that I realised just how significant that influence has been. Cheney School, founded by JHB, was my school of choice on passing the Eleven Plus exam. My father was also a craftsman, a printer, and I was taught by teachers who had been appointed by JHB, including Arnold Wainwright, an outstanding headmaster. After leaving school, I completed the Foundation Year at the Oxford School of Art, then part of the renamed Oxford College of Technology.

I then spent three years in an industrial town, in my case Manchester, studying design as had JHB. Whilst JHB's career centred on the world of education, my career developed in the commercial world, practising and then managing design, and running my own business. Having benefited from excellent teaching in my student days, I felt a debt of gratitude to education, and from early on in my career, I spent time lecturing, examining and mentoring students at design colleges. On re-reading some of my lecture notes, I realise that many of the ideas that I thought were mine, are drawn from JHB's ideas, undoubtedly lodged in my subconscious. My experience illustrates the experiences of a generation, hugely influenced, often unknowingly, through shared values and principles.

I was once asked if there were there any 'skeletons in the cupboard'. After several years of researching JHB's life, I can say that I have never come across anyone so universally respected, admired and loved.

A CHAMPAGNE MOMENT

In the early 1990s the Government of the day decided that polytechnics should be given university status. The designated institutions were required to register a name with the Privy Council. Certain words, like 'new', were not permitted. For Oxford Polytechnic it was not a straightforward task, given that it had a global university brand on the doorstep. The ancient university needed to be consulted, but having Oxford in the title was felt to be indisputable through longstanding prior use. Because of this challenging context, the institution was late in the timetable to get a name agreed and most of the other new universities had already settled their new names. The governors had decided to put the challenge out to competition, to staff and others close to the Polytechnic. The reward for the successful suggestion was a magnum of champagne. Many names were suggested but none were thought entirely suitable so it was decided to enrol professional help.

I was intrigued, somewhat unsure about the task, but keen to renew my acquaintance with a place where I had studied 25 years before. My company, Marketplace Design, entered and won the competitive pitch to name the university and create a corporate visual identity. A small steering group made up of the Polytechnic Director, Clive Booth, now Sir Clive Booth, and an established governor, Danby Bloch, were to work with us. Our first task was to review the names that had been proposed in the competition. They were mostly geographic in origin, such as Headington, Cherwell, Isis, Oxfordshire, and indeed many new universities had taken this route. However that seemed to us to feel subordinate to the established town and city names of red brick and older universities. Another suggestion was taking the name and perhaps the sponsorship of the later-disgraced resident of Headington Hill Hall, Robert Maxwell. Wisdom prevailed with the decision not to name the university after a living person.

We undertook desk research into so-called modern universities, particularly in the United States. Several had proper names honouring their founding benefactors such as Johns Hopkins University and Brown University. We also felt that it was sensible to focus and make a virtue of the modern compared to the established, in contrast to the University of Oxford; examples such as MIT compared to Harvard come to mind. So a modern university with a proper name was our recommendation to the governors. Their response was: yes, good proposal, what's the name?

So the search intensified and we recommended two names. One was William Morris, commemorating the past student, car maker, industrialist and philanthropist, with the same name as one of the leaders of the Arts and Crafts Movement, alumnus of Exeter College, Oxford, and resident of Kelmscott, Oxfordshire. The other recommendation was John Henry Brookes, who most of the governors knew something about but whose legacy had faded. The steering team supported our stronger recommendation of the Brookes name, along with the proposal that the institution retained the word Oxford, which had been used since its 1865 foundation. The Board of Governors, the University of Oxford and the Privy Council were all in agreement. We designed the visual identity and set standards for the implementation. To celebrate the new status and name, a small ceremony was held in Oxford Town Hall by the invitation of the Lord Mayor, John Power. The Polytechnic Director, who was to become the first Vice-Chancellor, Clive Booth, the Chairman of the Governors and Oxford East MP, Andrew Smith, and several governors and councillors attended. I was presented with the magnum of champagne and my firm was paid its fee.

The champagne moment; the author receiving a magnum of champagne for naming the University from the Oxford Polytechnic/Oxford Brookes University Chairman of Governors, Andrew Smith MP at a ceremony at the Oxford Town Hall in 1992.

Some time later, a formal opening ceremony was held where Joan Brookes unveiled a bronze sculpture of her father by the eminent Royal Academician and past member of staff, Leonard McComb, and an excellent exhibition was curated by staff member Ann Edmunds, which celebrated and displayed the life and work of JHB.

After my involvement in 1992, I stayed in touch with Oxford Brookes University on a more regular basis. When the University kindly made me an Honorary Fellow in 2005, they in time of course asked me to reciprocate the kindness and give a public lecture. Having recommended that the new university should take JHB's name, I became rather irked when people, knowing that I was associated with the place, asked why it was called Brookes. So I decided to research his life for a lecture in 2009 and launch a campaign to re-assert a fading legacy. I was determined that his vision and values should not be lost either to the University that bears his name or to the citizens of Oxford to whom he had devoted his life.

Over recent years, following the public lecture, we have achieved an Oxfordshire Blue Plaque on the house where JHB lived for 46 years, a number of newspaper and radio articles and a splendid posthumous portrait painted by the eminent portrait painter and alumnus, Anthony Morris. The family of Sir Kenneth Wheare, one of JHB's greatest Oxford supporters, recently revealed that both Wheare and JHB each thought the new College in Headington should include a building named after the other. In 2014, the new John Henry Brookes Building on the Headington Campus opened.

John Henry Brookes is the spiritual founder of Oxford Brookes University. His ideas and values are embedded in its DNA and the daily work of the University reflects what he aimed to achieve. Oxford and the modern University should be very proud of the spiritual founder.

JHB's daughter Joan unveiling the sculpture of her father made by Leonard McComb RA, to the right, at the celebratory launch of Oxford Brookes University in 1993 with Clive Booth, the University's first Vice-Chancellor, to the left.

APPENDICES

CHRONOLOGY

1865 Oxford School of Art founded

1891 Oxford City Council took over management of the institution, renamed Oxford City Technical School incorporating the School of Art

1891 John Henry Brookes (JHB) born on 31 January 1891

1903 JHB goes to Northampton Grammar School

1905 JHB moves to Wyggeston Grammar School, Leicester

1907 JHB moves to Leicester Municipal Training College

1909-13 JHB studies at Leicester Municipal Technical and Art School where he wins several scholarships

1910 JHB works part-time moving to full-time (1913) as a teaching assistant at Leicester Municipal Technical and Art School

1913 Morris Motors factory opens at Cowley

1914-18 World War One

1913-15 JHB attends the Summer School of the Guild of Handicraft, Chipping Campden

1916 JHB leaves Leicester, part-qualified in the principles and practice of teaching and school management, to work as a farm worker and live at Holly Bush Farm, Broad Campden after registering as a Conscentious Objector

1919 JHB marries Helena Victoria Mary Tyack on 7 October 1919.
JHB works as a studio assistant to the sculptor/carver Alec Miller in Chipping Campden and lives in Elm Bank Cottage, Broad Campden

1920 Daughter Joan born 30 September 1920

1923 Son Peter born 2 February 1923

1923-24 JHB works as Acting Principal of the Oxford School of Art and during the year receives an Art Teacher's Diploma

1924 JHB becomes Art Master at Penistone Grammar School, Sheffield, Yorkshire and teaches and takes courses at Sheffield University. During the year he receives a certificate of recognition as a Principal Teacher of a School of Art

1928 JHB appointed Deputy Principal of the Oxford City Technical School and Head of the School of Art with two staff and 90, mostly part-time students

1929 JHB and family move into the Gate House, 195 The Slade, Headington, Oxford; Commencement of classes in architecture and printing

1933 JHB is commissioned to carve the portico of St Alban's Church, Charles St, Oxford

1934 JHB becomes Principal of the renamed Oxford Schools of Technology, Art and Commerce with 10 full-time staff and 1,284 students. The Junior Technical School is founded

1935 JHB receives an Honorary MA from the University of Oxford

1939 Around 10,000 people are employed in the Oxford motor industry

1939-45 World War Two

1939 JHB elected President of the Oxford Rotary Club (Chairman 1945-46)

1941 First stage of a new engineering block at new premises at Cowley Road opened as a Ministry of Labour Training Centre

1943 JHB appointed Emergency Information Officer for Oxford City

1946 JHB appointed a Magistrate

1949 City Council acquires 33 acres on Headington Hill from the Morrell Estate for a new College building

1950 Plans for new College building rejected by the City Council; meeting of citizens to protest. The School of Architecture is fully recognised by The Royal Institute of British Architects (RIBA).

1952 Revised plans for the new College building approved by Oxford City Council. JHB has a painting accepted at the Royal Academy Summer Exhibition

1953 JHB awarded an OBE

1954 Lord Nuffield lays the Foundation Stone of the new College buildings at Headington. The Junior Technical School moves to the same site and becomes Cheney School

1956 JHB retires as Principal of the renamed Oxford College of Technology

1957 JHB commences publishing drawings in *The Oxford Times*

1960 JHB produces the first of five books, *Odds and Ends*, published and printed at the College

1961 JHB becomes Chief Magistrate

1963 Official opening of the new College buildings at Headington by the Duke of Edinburgh

1970 The College of Technology becomes Oxford Polytechnic

1975 JHB develops cancer and his excellent health declines; he dies in the Churchill Hospital on 29 September

ACKNOWLEDGEMENTS

This book has been written at the suggestion of the management team at Oxford Brookes University following my public lecture there in April 2009. I am grateful for the help of many people at the University, particularly my editor Susie Baker for her encouragement, enthusiasm and wise advice, and designer Victoria Mackintosh for her judgement and co-operation.

I'd also like to thank photographers Bob Pomfret and Lisa Hill; Archivist of the University Special Collections Eleanor Possart for her research; David Plant and other members of the library staff; Peter Forsaith for his research, Vice-Chancellor Janet Beer for kindly writing the introduction, and many colleagues for their good nature, enthusiastic interest and help with sources, including Hannah Marsh, Anna Myers and Jane Hobden for her proof reading.

The main source of personal insights came from my dear friend, the late Joan Brookes who so thoughtfully cared for her father's artwork, papers and legacy. I am also grateful to JHB's grandson Joachim Brookes and to Ruth Tuckwell, Helena Brookes's cousin.

My initial research was greatly helped by a retired member of the University library staff, Ann Edmunds. The early years were informed by research at the archives of De Montfort University, Leicester.

JHB's Guild of Handicraft years were informed by the Court Barn Museum in Chipping Campden, particularly Frank Johnson, Janice Fisher and Alan Crawford who kindly researched the Ashbee Journals at King's College, Cambridge for references to JHB. Also thanks are due to Graham Peel for research assistance and particularly for references to JHB's friendship with Alec Miller; Rebecca Nesbit, Keeper of the Jane Wilgress Trust and Alec Miller's great granddaughter, for permission to quote from JHB's letter to Alec Miller (page 29); Richard Russell for references to the Hart family, and Carol Jackson of CADHAS.

JHB's Oxford story was enriched by the following: Ken Brookfield, John Broadhurst, Nick Clack, Barbara Cleary, Malcolm Graham, Dennis Hall, Derek Holt, A E Jenkinson, Jenifer Lenton, Anthony Morris, *Oxford Mail* and *The Oxford Times*/Newsquest Oxfordshire Archivist Chris McDowell and past members of staff Don Chapman and John Chipperfield, the late John Payne, the late Chris Rayson (son of Tom), Hilary Stenning (née Kohler), Bernard Stone, Alan Walker, Tony White and many of JHB's past students and colleagues.

With regard to JHB's art, craft work and teaching, I am grateful to Alfonso De La Torre for information about Pablo Palazuelo and to the artist Janet Boulton for critical opinions.

Finally I want to thank my wife Buzz for living with another man for several years, and for her advice and encouragement whenever it has been needed.

SOURCES AND SELECT BIBLIOGRAPHY

As noted in the text, one of JHB's remarkable talents was that of administrator. No doubt born from the necessity of keeping records of his myriad activities, he filed material methodically. Hence there are two sources for researching JHB's life.

The main source is the John Henry Brookes Collection and the University History Collection, both housed in the Special Collections Archive at the Oxford Brookes University library. This contains many of JHB's files related to the development of the institution; press cuttings, institutional papers and photographs which he deposited following his retirement.

The second source is the Brookes family papers, most of which were preserved by his daughter Joan who died in 2011. She kindly gave and loaned me many of these files which will be deposited in the Special Collections Archive at the University. Other papers and artefacts reside with JHB's grandson Joachim Brookes.

The text includes a number of quotations from these sources and from some of the following books:

Books related to JHB's life and the history of Oxford Brookes University:

John Henry Brookes Craftsman Educator Administrator; a memorial to the life and work of John Brookes in Oxford 1928 to 1975, contributed by his friends and colleagues. Edited by A Stuart Addison, Oxford Polytechnic Press 1979

Genesis to Maturity 1865-1980 Elaine Henry, Oxford Polytechnic 1980

JHB's own books are partly autobiographical and provide useful source material:
Odds and Ends 1960; ***Time Off*** 1967; ***Country Corners in Oxfordshire*** 1969, published and printed at the Oxford College of Technology. ***Mid Oxfordshire Churches*** 1970 and ***North Oxfordshire Churches*** 1975, published by BCA Publications.

Other publications which are relevant to JHB's life include the following:
We Will Not Fight, Will Ellsworth-Jones, Aurum Press 2008

Arnold Wainwright, Peter Holmes and Philip Jones, Cheney School 1971*

Form and Civilization, Collected Papers on Art and Labour, William Richard Lethaby, Oxford University Press 1922, reprinted by BiblioLife LLC

The Simple Life, C R Ashbee in the Cotswolds, Fiona MacCarthy, Lund Humphries London 1981

William Morris, A life for our time, Fiona MacCarthy, Faber and Faber 1994

Tradition in Sculpture, Alec Miller, The Studio Publications; 1949

Alec Miller Carver Guildsman Sculptor; Graham Peel, published by Graham Peel 2014*

The Harts of Chipping Campden, Richard Russell, Harts Gold and Silversmiths 2008*

Alec Miller Guildsman and Sculptor in Chipping Campden, Jane Wilgress, Camden and District Historical and Archaeological Society 1987*

* Books containing specific references to JHB

INSTITUTION TITLES

Since its foundation in 1865, the institution has had many different names reflecting a changing organisation. Alternative names were used colloquially and for different occasions which meant that the corporate identity was not as consistent as it is today.
The following list offers a guide:

1865	Oxford School of Art
1870	Oxford School of Science and Art
1891	Oxford City Technical School
1928	Oxford City Technical School incorporating the School of Arts and Crafts
1934	Oxford Schools of Technology, Art and Commerce
1953	Oxford College of Technology, Art and Commerce
1956	Oxford College of Technology
1970	Oxford Polytechnic
1992	Oxford Brookes University

PICTURE CREDITS

The images in this book are reproduced by kind permission of the following lenders. All artworks made by John Henry Brookes are reproduced by kind permission of the copyright holder, his grandson Joachim Brookes. *Pictures by page numbers.*

Author: *78*, *85*; Court Barn, Chipping Campden (a project of the Guild of Handicraft Trust): *22 far right*; Hilary Stenning (née Kohler): *65*; Jean Roberts, portrait of the author: *inside back flap*; Joachim Brookes: *76/77*; National Portrait Gallery, London: *22 right*; Oxford Brookes University: *cover*, *inside front cover*, *2*, *8*, *10*, *15*, *17*, *18*, *19*, *24*, *25*, *26*, *28*, *33 both*, *34*, *35*, *38*, *40*, *41*, *45 below*, *46*, *47*, *48*, *49*, *52*, *53*, *55*, *56 right*, *56 both*, *58 right*, *58 both*, *59 both*, *61*, *62*, *63*, *66 both*, *68*, *70*, *73*, *74 both*, *75*, *79*, *81*, *82 all*, 83, 84 *all*, *87*, *90*, *91*, *back cover*; also from Oxford Mail and Times/Newsquest: *41*, *45 below*, *46*, *47*, *53*, *56*, *58*, *59*, *61*, *68*, *83*, *91*; Paul Tait: *inside back cover*; Pablo Palazuelo Foundation, Azcona Foundation, courtesy of Alfonso de la Torre: *45 left*; Rebecca Nesbit, Keeper of the Jane Wilgress Trust, on loan to The Wilson, Cheltenham's art gallery and museum: *30*; Rector and scholars of Exeter College at the University of Oxford: *43 left*; Ruth Tuckwell: *20*; Stephanie Jenkins: *36*; Topfoto: *43 far left*.

INDEX

Note: Page numbers in ***bold italics*** refer to illustrations.

Acland, Sir Henry 36
Addison, Stuart, *John Henry Brookes Craftsman Educator Administrator* 69, ***70***
applied education *see* technical education
architecture *see also* School of Architecture
  JHB's interest in 80
  JHB initiating study of 39-40, 43
art school training 18, 23, 74, 83, 86
Arts and Crafts Movement 21-2
  influence on JHB 22-7, 74, 83,
  see also Guild of Handicraft
Arts Guild ***82***
Ashbee, Charles ***22***, 23, 27, 43
Ashmolean Museum, 37

Bailey, Cyril 46
Barnsley, Ernest and Sidney 25
Batey, Charles 39, 60
Blackwell, Sir Basil 31, 67, 69
Blenheim Palace 80
Bloch, Danby 89
Blue Plaque 41, 91
Booth, Sir Clive 89, 90, ***91***
Broadhurst, Charles 67
Brookes, Annie (née Dykes) ***15***, 16
Brookes, Helena (née Tyack) 30, ***33***, 41, 64, ***68***, ***79***
Brookes, Joan 31, 32, 41, 48, 64, ***68***, ***79***, 91, ***91***
Brookes, Joachim 64
Brookes, John Henry
  accolades and appreciations 46, 51, 67, 69-70
  as actor 44, ***45***
  as artist and craftsman 31, 74-86; *see also* drawings *and* paintings *see below*
  books 80, ***82***
  building named after 61, 91
  career: as Miller's studio assistant 29, 30, 32; wartime farm work 29; as teacher 32; as Head of Oxford School of Arts and Crafts 11-12, 31, 32-4, 39-44; as Principal of Oxford Schools of Technology, Arts and Commerce 44-62
  carving 29, 75
  chronology of life 92-3
  on College of Technology foundation 61-2
  community activities 64-9
  as conscientious objector 28-9, 32, 67
  designs 80, ***81***, ***82***
  drawings 75, 80; bookplate design ***74***; Chipping Campden ***24***; Church Street buildings ***8***, ***34***, ***38***, ***52***; family tree ***17***; Gate House ***40***, 41; greetings cards ***74***; Headington site ***58***; Joan Brookes ***33***; male head ***20***; memorial ***84***; Oxford City Arms ***81***, ***82***; pastoral scene ***84***; Rozel Harbour ***85***; St Mary's Church, Iffley ***84***;
  education and training 18-21, 24, 31, 74, 83, 86
  educational philosophy, 50
  magistrate 67
  marriage and family life 30, 41, 64
  modern art, views on 83
  OBE ***68***, 69
  organisational memberships 64-9
  on Oxford College of Technology opening 69
  paintings: plant study ***19***; St Giles' Church 75, ***78***; wife and daughter (cartouche) ***79***
  Oxford, involvment in life of 64-9
  personal values 88
  photographs of ***2***, ***15***, ***18***, ***25***, ***35***, ***48-9***, ***56***, ***63***, ***65***, ***66***, ***68***, ***73***, ***83***, ***87***
  portrait of ***10***
  post-retirement activities 67-9, 80
  recollection, Bryan Brown's 89
  retirement 62, 64
  sculpture of ***91***
  silversmithing 25, 75, ***76-77***
  teaching skills 31, 44
  University named after 88, 89-91
  wartime duties 48
Brookes, Margaret ***15***, 41
Brookes, Peter 31, 41, 48, 64
'Brookes Pulpit' 42
Brookes, Robert Henry ***15***, 16, 28, ***28***, 74
Brookes family ***15***, 16, ***17***
Brown, Bryan
  Prologue 11
  JHB's influence on 88-9
  naming of University 90, ***90***
business education 50

Cameron, A C 11, 39
Carrington, Noel 42

Cave, Reginald 51
Central School of Arts and Crafts 27
Cheney School 12, 46, 62, 89
Chipping Campden 22, 23, 24, ***24***, 25, ***26***, 75
Church Street premises 37, 38-9, 54, 62, 67
  JHB's drawings of ***8***, ***34***, ***38***, ***52***
City and Guilds of London Institute 37
Clarke, Kenneth (later Lord) 42
conscientious objector 28-9, 32, 67
Cotswold School 23, 25
Coventry Cathedral 29, ***30***
Cowley Road premises 47, ***48***, 52, 55, 60
Crossland, Bernard 80

Dale, Thomas Lawrence 40
design
  education in 27, 89
  JHB's skills 80, ***81***, ***82***
Dig for Victory campaign 48
Dono, George 54, 60
Doré, Paul Gustave 18
Doric Club 40, 44, 57
drawings *see under* Brookes, John Henry

Edinburgh, Duke of 69
Edmunds, Ann 91
education
  in design 27, 89
  and industry 36-8, 50, 51-2
  JHB's educational philosophy 50; on education for industry and commerce in Oxford 51-2; influence of Arts and Crafts movement 27; on integration of artistic and technical subjects 43, 46, 57; on social activities 44, 64
  see also technical education
Education Act (1902) 37
engineering 46, 47, 48, 54

Fielding Dodd, Ronald 40
Flemming, Arthur 31
Fletcher, Benjamin ***18***, 25, 50
footwear manufacture 16

Garne, John 12
Gate House ***40***, 41, 64
Gill, Eric 26, 75
Gimson, Ernest 25
Griggs, Fred 26, ***26***, 29, 84
Grimshaw, Reginald 51, 54
Guild of Handicraft
  influence on JHB 22-7, 34, 44, 50, 64, 74, 75, 88
  summer schools 24, 25, ***25***, 75
Guild of Handicraft Trust 24, 29

Hart, George 24, 25, ***25***, 29, 32, 75
Hart, Will 32
Headington Hill site 55, 57-60, 58
Henry, Elaine *Genesis to Maturity 1865-1980* 69
Holly Bush Farm 29, 74

industrialisation 16, 21
industry and education 36-8, 50, 51-2

Jenkinson, A Edward 12
John Henry Brookes Building 61, 91
Johnson, Dr John 39, 42
Junior Technical School 46, 62

Keene, Edgar 32
Kelly, George 54, 60
Kelmscott Manor 23, 26
Kensington system 36
Kohler, Basil ***65***, 83

Leicester School of Art 18, ***18***, 25, 74, 86
Lethaby, William 27, 50

Liddell, Sir Henry 36

Marlborough, Duke of 36
Magistrate, Chief 67
Maxwell, Robert 90
McComb, Leonard 91, ***91***
Milham Ford School 41, 52
Miller, Alec 25-6, 29, ***30***, 31, 32, 75, 83
Morrell family 36, 55
Morris, Anthony, portrait by ***10***, 91
Morris, G W 32
Morris, May 21, 26
Morris, William (artist and craftsman) 21, ***22***, 39, 50, 90
Morris, William (later Lord Nuffield) 38, 55, 60, 61, ***61***, 90

Natural History Museum 37
Northampton 16, 18

Nuffield, Lord (William Morris) 38, 55, 60, 61, ***61***, 90
Nuffield Organisation 51, 54, 57

Oxford Art School Players 44, ***45***
Oxford Brookes University 61, 88, 89-91
Oxford City Arms ***81***, ***82***
Oxford City Council 37, 55, 61
  rejection of proposed college 57-60
Oxford City Technical School 34, 37-8
  see also Oxford Schools of Technology, Art and Commerce
Oxford College of Further Education (City of Oxford College) 12, 55, 60
Oxford College of Technology, Art and Commerce 60, 61, ***61***, 62
Oxford College of Technology 69
Oxford Education Committee 11, 12, 37, 40, 42, 43, 47, 54, 57, 59, 60, 67
Oxford Mail ***41***, ***47***, ***53***, ***56***, ***58***, ***59***, ***60***, ***61***, ***83***
Oxford Polytechnic 69
  university status 89-90
Oxford Rotary Club ***66***, 67
Oxford School of Art
  appointment of JHB 11-12, 31, 32, 34
  eminent visitors 42
  expansion 44
  foreign students 43-4
  foundation 9, 11, 36-37
  new areas of study *see* architecture; printing
  premises inadequacy 36, 37, 38-9
  social activities 44, ***45***, 64
  see also Oxford Schools of Technology, Art and Commerce
Oxford School of Science and Art 37
Oxford Schools of Technology, Art and Commerce
  formation and expansion 44, 46, 47, 57
  governors 54
  inspection 57
  new site: planning 55, 57; City Council's rejection 57-60
  post-war courses 52
  premises 47, 52-5
  staff photographs ***35***, 66
  wartime courses 48
Oxford Spires Academy 12, 44
Oxford Times, The
  on rejection of technical college proposals 59
  JHB's drawings ***52***, 80
Oxford, University of 11, 37
  JHB's honorary MA 46
  support from 42-3, 47
  town/gown divide 37, 51
Oxford University Press 39, 42

pacificism 28-9
paintings *see under* Brookes, John Henry
Palazuelo, Pablo 43-4, ***45***
Penistone Grammar School 32
Pressed Steel Company 48, 54, 60
Printing, Department of 52, 80
Printing School 39
Protest at Oxford Town Hall 59-60

Randolph Galleries 37
Rayson, Thomas 31, 32, 40, 41, 80, 83
Reeve, Sydney ***18***, 25
Rhodes House 60
Royal Academy Summer Exhibition 75, ***78***
Royal Institute of British Architects 47, 56, 57
Ruskin, John 21, 23, 37

Sadler, Sir Michael 42, 47
St Alban's Church, Oxford 75, ***75***
St Giles' Church, Horspath 75, ***78***
St Hilda's College, Oxford 52
St Mary's Church, Iffley ***84***
School of Architecture 39-40, 43, 47, 52, ***56***, 57
  RIBA recognition 47, 56, 57
School of Handicraft 23, 27, 50
  summer schools 24, 25, ***25***, 75
science teaching 37, 46
scraper-board ***38***, ***52***, ***82***, 84, ***85***
Sheffield, University of 12, 32
silversmithing 25, 75, ***76-77***
Singletree House 57, ***66***
Smith, Andrew ***90***
social activities, importance 44, 64
Southfield School 12, 44
summer schools, School of Handicraft 24, 25, ***25***, 75

Taylor Institution 36, ***36***
technical education 11, 37-8, 50, 51-2, 59, 88

University Museum 37

vocational education *see* technical education

Wade, Kenneth 89
war memorials 29
Wainwright, Arnold ***35***, 36, 89
Wheare, Sir Kenneth 42, ***43***, 47, 57, 60, 69, 91
Williams-Ellis, Sir Clough 42, ***43***
Wood, Francis 31, 32
World War One 28-9
World War Two 12, 47, 48, 51, 52
Wyggeston Grammar School 18

Your Country Needs You campaign 28

Inside back cover: John Henry Brookes Building, Headington Campus Oxford Brookes University, 2015

Outside flap: Portrait of the author, Bryan Brown, by Jean Roberts